Practical Partners
A Service Dog Research Guide

Practical Partners
A Service Dog Research Guide

Julie Nye

Fieldstone Hill Press

Greenville, South Carolina

Practical Partners: A Service Dog Research Guide

Copyright © 2005 Julie Nye. All rights reserved. First edition 2005.

Published by Fieldstone Hill Press, P.O. Box 14729, Greenville, SC 29610. *www.fieldstone-hill.net*

Except for brief excerpts used in reviews, no part of this publication may be reproduced, transmitted, transcribed, or translated into any language or computer language, in any form or by any means, electronic or mechanical, including photocopy, recording, or any other information storage or retrieval system now in existence or yet to be invented, except by prior written permission of the author.

Author   Julie Nye

Editor   Susan B. Peck

Production Coordinator   Richard Peck

Cover Photos   Courtesy of Dogs for Disabled, Greenville, SC

Trademarks and Copyrights   Fieldstone Hill Press, and the Fieldstone Hill Press logo are trademarks of Fieldstone Hill Press. Frequent references within this book to training methods by Connie Cleveland are documented in various articles and publications copyrighted by Tara, Inc. Further information can be obtained from the web site *www.dogtrainersworkshop.com* or by writing to Dog Trainers Workshop, 207 Greenpond Road, Fountain Inn, SC 29644.

Notice   All discussion and suggestions about service dogs and related matters within this book are intended only as tools for use in your research and evaluation. In no case does this book's content replace the need for individual assessment and guidance from trainers, health professionals, and legal counsel; for safety and effectiveness, it is strongly suggested that you work closely with qualified, experienced individuals from each of those categories to discern the best solution to meet your individual needs.

ISBN: 0-9767762-0-0

Printed in the United States of America.
10 9 8 7 6 5 4 3 2 1

*In memory of my father,
Harold Nye,
the master of pragmatic questions*

Table of Contents

1	**Chapter 1: Pragmatic Standards**	
	WHY THIS BOOK?	3
	HOW TO USE THIS BOOK	5
7	**Chapter 2: Basic Concepts**	
	THE DOGS	8
	THE PEOPLE	9
	THE SETTING	10
	VARIETIES AND CLARIFICATION	10
	QUALIFICATION	12
	TASKS	14
	IN CONCLUSION	20
21	**Chapter 3: Dogs Are Not Furry People**	
	SOCIAL WORRIES	22
	SPECIFIC CONSIDERATIONS	27
31	**Chapter 4: Certification**	
	LEGAL SERVICE ANIMALS	32
	DEFINITION FROM U.S. DEPARTMENT OF JUSTICE	33
	WHAT IS CERTIFICATION?	34
	WHAT IS CERTIFICATION NOT?	37
	PRACTICAL CONSIDERATIONS	38
	EVALUATING CERTIFICATION	41
	PERSONAL RESPONSIBILITY	43
45	**Chapter 5: Understanding & Evaluating Training Methods**	
	COMPETENCE	46

TABLE OF CONTENTS

	TECHNIQUE	48
	COMMUNICATION GAP	50
	ASK QUESTIONS	53
	CORRECTIONS AND REWARDS	54
	CURRICULUM	55
	CHECKLIST	57
59	**Chapter 6: The Corrections Controversy**	
	CANINE CORRECTIONS	60
	TRENDS IN TIMES	61
	MOTIVATIONAL LIMITS	62
	PROBLEM AREAS	62
	PROBLEM TASKS	66
	SEPARATING WORK FROM SPORT	66
	TEACHING CORRECTIONS	68
	ELECTRIC COLLARS	72
	DECISIONS	74
77	**Chapter 7: The Job Description**	
	BREEDS AND JOBS	78
	REALISM	79
	TASKS	80
	INDIVIDUAL ACTIONS	81
	COMBINATIONS OF ACTIONS	83
	NON-REINFORCEABLE TASKS	91
	NON-OBSERVABLE ACTIONS	96
	TASK SORTING	98
	CHOOSE CAREFULLY	99
103	**Chapter 8: Service Dogs and Children**	
	PROS AND CONS	103
	ADOLESCENCE MAGNIFIED	104

	PACK ORDER	107
	PARENTAL CONSIDERATIONS	108
	TECHNICALITIES	112
	TAKE YOUR TIME	113
115	**Chapter 9: Breeds**	
	PERSONALITY	116
	TEMPERAMENT WITHIN PERSONALITY	116
	TRAINER RATIONALE	117
	RESEARCH	118
	PREDISPOSITIONS	119
	SIZE	121
	MINDSET	123
	FINAL CONSIDERATIONS	133
135	**Chapter 10: Obtaining Dogs**	
	RESCUES	135
	BREEDING PROGRAMS	137
	BUYING FROM A BREEDER	139
	PRE-OWNED DOGS	140
143	**Chapter 11: Evaluating Temperament**	
	CRITERIA FOR ANALYSIS	143
	UNPLANNED TESTS	144
	PLANNED TESTS	146
	GENETIC PREDISPOSITION	153
	TESTS IN THE PAST	155
157	**Chapter 12: Legal Considerations**	
	LIABILITY	158
	INSURANCE	158
	ACCESS	159

TABLE OF CONTENTS

	TRAINEES	161
	BREED-SPECIFIC RESTRICTIONS	162
	EMPLOYMENT	162
	CONTRACTS	165
169	**Chapter 13: Resident Therapy Dogs**	
	SELECTION	171
	CAREFUL INTRODUCTION	173
	HANDLERS	173
	PROTECTION	174
	SPECIFIC CONSIDERATIONS	175
179	**Chapter 14: ASA Dogs**	
	MULTIPLE FUNCTIONS	180
	DEMANDING ROLE	184
	POTENTIAL VARIATIONS	187
	EXPERIENCE REQUIRED	187
191	**Chapter 15: Programs and Opinions**	
	ACCOUNTABILITY	192
	CHECKS AND BALANCES	193
	NATIONAL REGISTRATION	195
	ENORMOUS EFFORTS	198
	INVERSE RATIOS	200
	THE CHALLENGE WE FACE	203
205	**Appendix A: When Personality Meets Character**	
	CONTEXT	207
	HISTORY	207
	THE PROCESS	209
	THE TITLE	211
	THE EVALUATION	213

JOB VARIETY	217
BASIC CONFIDENCE	221
ESSENCE OF THE TEST	222
CAUTION	223
APPLICATION	224
NEGATIVE ASSOCIATIONS	227
PROTECTION DOGS ARE NOT SERVICE DOGS	230
CONCLUSION	231

235   Index

Acknowledgements

Writing acknowledgments can be a more daunting task than the book itself. In truth, it would be impossible to note every contributor to *Practical Partners* since the first tentative outline went on paper almost ten years ago. Nearly every client, every dog-training friend, every sponsor, every fellow service dog trainer—and even every dog—has made his own addition to detail and perspective. In fact, that very synthesis of need, question, and opinion entirely defined this book's content. It's not possible to mention each one, or even a few score of the most important. As press time looms, I can only remember my debt of gratitude to so many: their time, shared thoughts, patience with my errors, and honest critiques. However, here in this short section, it's especially important to remember several who played the largest roles.

Of course, from the beginning, Brian and Connie Cleveland initially transformed my interest in service dogs from intrigue to involvement. I am forever indebted to them for spending resources and time developing the Dogs for Disabled program, and also for providing so much training to me and others, thus creating the foundation for all that followed. Without their efforts there would have been no program, no trainers, no starting place, and no book. Throughout *Practical Partners*, you will encounter references to Connie's training methods which have endured for years and proven their effectiveness with thousands of clients and many types of dogs. I am grateful for her permission to refer to them so frequently.

In the long quest for adequate expertise, no single person has had a more profound effect on my training philosophy and approach to distinguishing canine personality than Chris Elliott. In the early years, I have no idea how many hours we spent watching each other work various dogs, nor how many hours we spent discussing and dissecting the work. A lot. But from that friendship, her patience with me, her enormous talent, and her dedication to specific analysis came my first real understanding of adaptability in training procedures—which is the very essence of advanced work with assistance dogs. Almost all subsequent events have been much shaped by Chris's influence; without it I'm not sure I would ever have arrived at the level of objectivity needed to write this book.

Beyond that, over the years, many other dog trainers have helped me think through and sort out techniques, temperament issues, and effective training styles as they relate to the material in this book—both for the dogs and for the people. No others have put more hours into this effort than Isabel Lambertz and Christopher Perry, especially as concerns Chapter 11 and the related Appendix. Many thanks to both of them for helping me figure out how best to present a difficult topic.

Regardless of need, talent, ability, or willingness, almost all modern endeavors run hard up against a brick wall called reality; the business concerns of a major publishing effort are both demanding and unforgiving. To Paul MacDonald goes the credit for applying a realistic framework, providing answers to nonstop practical questions, and ensuring that the entire project did not self-destruct before it ever made it to the printer. Without his input, *Practical Partners* would undoubtedly still be wandering in the never-never land of great ideas that couldn't "get there."

To Norma Nye and Sherry Brown go the purple-heart awards for combat in the publishing trenches. They helped with the project on a daily basis: encouraging, listening, chiding, critiquing, proofreading, and otherwise putting up with me during the production months. To both goes my heartfelt gratitude for enduring—and for not buying cross-continent tickets to more tranquil pastures, abandoning me to my fate. I'm sure the temptation was there.

In this section, last is not least, but largest. All known phrases fall short when I attempt to capsulize the involvement from Dick and Susan Peck. Their input to *Practical Partners* went so far beyond the call of friendship as to defy describing. Decades of expertise in publishing and extreme graciousness of spirit both played roles to transform this book from the conceptual to the actual. Their dedication and generosity—and their priceless friendship—are matters at which I can only marvel and be thankful for. From the thought concepts to the press run, the Pecks made major, essential contributions at every stage, donating their time and professionalism to be editors, public relations specialists, project analysts, content evaluators, and print researchers—not to mention being the frequent hotline for a generally frustrated author. Their efforts brought all the other contributions together into a finished product. Whatever good comes of *Practical Partners* is at least as much to their credit as my own. But for their timely intervention, the goal of many years would still be a goal, not a book.

To all readers, please know that any value you find was made possible by those mentioned here. To all contributors, I am grateful beyond words for your help. It is my hope that the results of this book will, of themselves, provide a means of thanks far greater than my limited ability to express.

Julie Nye
Greenville, SC
May 2005

Special Note

Every effort has been made to include accurate and current references within this book. However, due to the fluid nature of the World Wide Web, some of the references to various web sites are certain to change over time. In an attempt to provide all possible resources, Fieldstone Hill Press will maintain a list of links and references on our web site, *www.fieldstonehill.net,* including those in this book, and do our best to keep them current for your use.

We would encourage you to visit our web site for additional information and tools as you continue your adventure with service dogs. In the months ahead, we will be adding information such as sample checklists, scoresheets, contracts, training outlines, and questionnaires, which will be available for your use, free of charge.

Thank you for your interest in service dogs, and may you experience every success!

Chapter 1:

Pragmatic Standards

So you want a service dog? Or perhaps you want to help someone else get a service dog? If so, you're probably holding this book in your hands because you've already discovered what a confusing project it can be. It's highly unlikely *Practical Partners* will answer every question you have. No single book could possibly be a comprehensive authority on such a topic, but perhaps this one can give you a quick foundation and get you started in the right direction for additional help. However, to make this book a useful tool, you should keep in mind two extremely important factors.

First, *dogs do not do not fit very well into unqualified statements and categories.* Every "rule" in the world has exceptions, but most "dog rules" have a dozen exceptions. This is partly because of the widely varied nature of domestic canines themselves, and partly because their personalities and behavior are tremendously influenced by people—who are just as different as the dogs. Consequently, a book containing specific information is forced to do a certain amount of generalizing, lest every sixth or seventh word in the text be "usually" or "often" and the finished product weigh 10 pounds. Keep in mind from the beginning that you are reading about averages and commonalities—the more central highlights of major issues. Think of the principles explored in this book not as absolutes, but as trends. Each particular dog must be investigated to see exactly where he fits into the spectrum.

The second factor is even more important: *when dealing with disabilities, generalization almost does not exist at all*. Each situation is absolutely unique. Yes, disabilities are named and categorized, but not a single one is exactly like any other. Nor are the life circumstances of the person involved. To apply an effective solution—including dogs, or perhaps especially dogs—one must always keep in mind that what works for one situation will not necessarily work for another. Of course the same principle is true in many fields, such as education, medicine, or advertising, but the concept is magnified when service animals are paired with disabled people. The increase of importance stems from the fact that the professional is not the only one who needs functional understanding.

Chemotherapy can do its job whether the patient understands the process or not. Many people who react to commercials do not understand why their psyches respond to the advertisement. But in the service dog training/placement process, the client must not only understand, but also agree and cooperate. He or she is attempting to control and direct another sensate, intelligent being. Those facts, by necessity, put the individual (or perhaps the parent) in the driver's seat for the major decisions. He knows the specific situation better than anybody else—which translates to a burden of self-education. Each individual must retain both the initiative and responsibility to determine the best solution to pursue.

With those two factors in mind, I urge you to read with a constantly critical mindset, evaluating each concept for how—or if—it applies to your needs and circumstances. I present this material solely for informational and educational purposes, not in any way presuming or suggesting to know what is best for you. What is "best" is not something any book can tell you; that is not only an individual's right, but also his responsibility.

WHY THIS BOOK?

Practical Partners has been underway for more than a decade, except that in the earlier years, I didn't realize exactly what I was working on. My fascination with assistance dogs began somewhere around 1987 when I met a young man and his German Shepherd assistance dog in a park. A few more years passed before I became more formally involved. However, as my first interest sparked efforts at reading and research, almost immediately I realized there wasn't a whole lot of written information. I was a little slow realizing that the individualized nature of disabilities defies most attempts to make tidy outlines.

The desire for guidance is very understandable. The need is immense, the task is important, and the situations are incredibly varied and complex. After a trainer has finished his first few trainees and the landslide of new requests begins, the vast complications will have him ripping out his hair in handfuls. No trainer, no program, no advisor can begin to understand fully the nature and implications of one single disability in the way that the individual himself, and/or his immediate family, is forced to understand. How much more true for a collection of scores of clients? Because, as said, the people and the situations are all different. Very different. And so are the dogs.

On the other side of this equation are some people whose lives have not only been "turned upside down" by a disability—their lives have been flipped, shaken, and rolled down a hill. Others have been fighting limitations since birth—constant challenges about which most of the population never has a clue.

When some of these folks decide the concept of a service dog merits exploration, "frustration" can be a sadly inadequate term to describe the onslaught of widely varied, or even completely conflicting, information. Ten phone calls or interviews later, such people might be more confused than when they started researching. Is the whole idea of getting a service dog wonderful or terrible? Even deciding that much alone can be an exasperating project.

    I have always been more writer than trainer. As I gained experience, my natural reaction was to think, "I have to get this information written up to provide some reading material. It would be easier for me as well as others." Single sheets became stapled handouts, then booklets, then notebooks. Each time I would think I was getting some concepts defined, some new situation would come along and blast half of my operating principles right out of the water.

    As the years inched past, I realized the wisdom of those who drafted our federal legislation about people with disabilities: every situation has to be considered on a case-by-case basis. At that point, I began to understand that the need for a starter handbook was not about giving people a list of answers. It was about helping them understand the questions. Information does not have to be universally comprehensive to be correct and helpful. Over the years, I learned of too many people—for lack of knowing even the correct questions to ask—making inappropriate choices of dogs, too many sponsors paying for inadequate training, and too many situations where people with disabilities were settling for a fraction of the help they really could have had. *Practical Partners* grew from the desire that fewer people would have such experiences, that more people would have an objective basis for self-guidance.

HOW TO USE THIS BOOK

Thus, as my involvement with the service dog world changes focus from training to education, I hope to help others avoid the lumps I acquired in the school of hard knocks. I've heard an old saying in several places: "most serious errors seemed like a good idea at the time." Yes, they did! But all the best intentions didn't lessen the severity of some of my more monumental screwups. Beyond that, the majority of my errors were those of omission, rather than commission—factors I simply failed to consider at all. If you are looking for a book on the mechanics of training a service dog, this is not it. Bookstores already have a wealth of training information that I could not possibly duplicate. *Practical Partners* is about how to plan a merger between the world of working dogs and the nature of individual disabilities.

The acronym FAQ, which stands for frequently asked questions, is almost universally understood today. A huge percentage of Internet web sites have a section devoted to FAQs. Essentially, this book is a rather expanded FAQ, representing my point of view on the common questions I have been asked uncountable times over the years. It's critical to stress that I do not speak for the program, Dogs For Disabled, with which I have been affiliated for more than a decade. Many examples arise from my work there. Many specifics refer to that program's practices or policies and how they came to be. But *Practical Partners* is an entirely private work, based on experiences both within and outside of the Dogs For Disabled program.

As such, I have no delusions that each reader will agree with every element presented. Far from it. I'm certain everyone can find something about which to disagree! I honestly hope you do, because if you know what you do and don't agree with—that tells me you're putting serious thought into the process and not just reading to obtain a list of fool-proof instructions (of which there is no such thing!). What percentage you agree with me is less important than the need to hold an extremely pragmatic standard. People living with disabilities need solutions, not rhetoric. In the end, if you disagree with every point made in this book, if your response to every suggestion is the knowledge that it wouldn't work for you, if you discover that I've raised a question but failed to include significant information…then the book will still have served much of its purpose by helping you define and refine what is practical, safe, and helpful for your own circumstances.

Whether you are considering a service dog for your own use or for another's use, or whether you want to learn how to train the dog, or breed the dog, or buy the dog, I hope to get you started with enough information for critical analysis. I encourage you to read with a pen in hand. Don't trust your memory, but make notes as you go. Let's get started…and happy researching. May your solution with a service dog be the most effective and rewarding project you've ever undertaken.

Chapter 2:

Basic Concepts

 When does a dog become a service animal? How is that term different from assistance dog? And what do they do? Before we even start trying to define tasks, it's important to make sure, right from the beginning, that we define terms to use consistently when referring to animals, people, and functions in this book. First and foremost, this book addresses service dogs and related issues as they exist within the United States only. Other countries have different policies. The US Department of Justice defines a service animal as any animal that has been specifically and individually trained to assist a particular person with his or her disability.[1] Such a definition includes different species of service animals, widely-varied disabilities, and many kinds of tasks. For our purposes, we need to narrow the focus.

---

[1] The definition of a service animal is from the U.S. Department of Justice's publication "Frequently Asked Questions About Service Animals in Places of Business," (FAX # 3204). The entire publication can be viewed online at *www.usdoj.gov/crt/ada/qasrvc.htm*.

THE DOGS

Various organizations use different terms to refer to service dogs and their functions. *Practical Partners* focuses primarily on service dogs who are trained to help people with tasks other than those related to vision and hearing. Dogs are classified according to the following definitions.

Service Dogs	A dog who has been specifically and individually trained to assist a person with a recognized disability of any kind. Disabled individuals have the right to be accompanied by this dog into any place that serves the public, even those with a no-pets policy. A service dog is not a pet. Service dogs are generally categorized into three groups:
Guide Dogs	Dogs trained to provide mobility assistance to those with vision impairment.
Hearing Assistance Dogs	Dogs trained to provide alerts to sounds for those with hearing impairment.
Assistance Dogs	Dogs trained to assist with disabilities other than blindness or deafness.
Companion Dogs	Dogs trained for any of the above categories, but intended for in-home use only, not for use in public settings.
Resident Therapy Dogs	Dogs trained to reside permanently in medical or caregiving facilities and to socialize and interact with the residents.

THE PEOPLE

Terms about people can be confusing, also. To clarify which human role we're referring to during each topic's discussion, here are some general definitions.

Client	The person with the disability who is seeking or using a service dog.
Program	A business or non-profit group whose primary concern is the training and placing of service animals with clients.
Trainer	The individual person (whether privately or as a member of a program) who is training a dog to perform as a service animal. Please note that any individual can train his own dog, therefore the client and the trainer could possibly be the same person in different roles.
Handler	The person who has control of the dog at any given moment, whether he be trainer, client, original owner, or a volunteer.
Parent	The parent or primary caregiver of a child with a disability.
Sponsor	An individual or a group who pays the expenses of training and placing a service dog with a disabled individual.

THE SETTING

Finally, let's make sure of a few terms related to places and practicalities.

Public	Any place a service dog performs his duties outside the home. Many of the settings are places where regular pets are not allowed, such as stores, office buildings, and theaters.
Home	The home of a person with a disability.
Kennel	The dog-residence section of a trainer's or program's business.
Trainee	A dog who is being trained for service dog work, but is not yet finished with his training.

VARIETIES AND CLARIFICATION

The concept of dogs assisting people with special jobs is hardly new. Guide dogs and dogs assisting with physical tasks have been mentioned in historical accounts long before our times. Guide dogs are only one kind of service animal, but probably the most widely known. Guide dogs have been recognized in the US since 1928, when Morris Frank brought his guide dog, Buddy, to this country from Switzerland. As a result, guide dogs have been commonly accepted around the United States for decades. Dogs who provide other types of assistance are a newer concept to most people; federal sanction of service animals is newer yet, having its origins in The Americans with Disabilities Act (ADA) of 1990.

    Furthermore, dogs are only one species of service animal. Monkeys are becoming increasingly common, particularly for quadriplegics with limited ability to move their hands. Miniature horses are also used for extensive help pulling wheelchairs—sometimes even for guide work! The tiny equines are particularly well suited for certain special circumstances, and their longevity makes them attractive for those who do not need a wide variety of tasks performed. They can also be extremely helpful filling the gap for someone who might be allergic to dogs. A horse is certainly trainable, but is not inclined either by disposition or by physical construction to perform some of the tasks that come more easily to dogs.

The term "service dog" can cause confusion, because many people also use the term to refer to police K9 units. Various groups have commonly used the term "assistance dog" rather than service dog, evident in the name of the voluntary accrediting group "Assistance Dogs International." Many people within the industry consider the terms interchangeable. As indicated in the list of terms above, I prefer the term "service dog," as designated by the US Department of Justice, to refer to all categories, with the distinction of "assistance dog" reserved for dogs that help with disabilities other than blindness or deafness.

For our discussions in this book, except where otherwise mentioned, the guide dog industry is entirely excluded. Guide dog schools have been established far longer than any other type of service dog work and, overall, I believe have an infrastructure far more advanced than most assistance dog groups. Moreover, guide dog training is an area in which I have never been involved, other than the occasional donated puppy, and have no perspective to share. Hearing assistance dogs are included to some degree, but I would stress that they, also, form their own subset of training, and my experience in training them is far more limited. Hearing assistance differs in substantial ways from dogs who perform physical tasks on direct cue from their handler. Moreover, so far as I can determine, more information is available in print about both guide and hearing assistance dogs than about assistance dogs for other disabilities.

QUALIFICATION

The most common concept of an assistance dog is one accompanying a person who uses a wheelchair. Though this is certainly a major category, it is by no means a requirement that the client use a chair. Many people use dogs for assistance with disabilities that are not visible. Quite commonly the disabling condition is not present 100% of the time, such as those related to seizures, brain injuries, Post Traumatic Stress Disorder, or Multiple Sclerosis. As mentioned in Chapter 1, the work of assistance dogs is extremely varied and extremely specific.

If an individual has a medically-recognized disability and a dog can be trained in such a way as to help with an essential life task (often referred to in legal language as a "major life activity") and thus make that task possible, easier, quicker, less painful, or more practical, then the dog has met the legal definition of a service animal.

However, that legal definition of "service animal" is also inseparable from the person with the disability. This principle is true particularly where public accommodation is concerned. If the dog is not engaged in the business of assisting the disabled person for whom he was trained, then he is for that time, *not* qualified as a service animal and is subject to the same restrictions as any other dog or pet. In other words, if you have a service animal and you choose not to take him on your family vacation, you cannot legitimately leave him with your sister whose apartment has a "no pets" policy. Unless you're there with him, he's not functioning as a service dog and therefore has no business in the apartment.

In fact, even those who train service dogs are under far greater limitations than the disabled individuals who actually own and use the dogs. A few states (including Florida and Arizona) have given supplemental recognition to trainers and dogs-in-training.[2] But at the federal level, the only dogs who are recognized as service animals are those whose training is complete and are presently working for a person with a disability. Trainers working their canine students are, in most cases, required to get permission from the owners or authorities of public places to have the trainees on the premises.

Finally, from a legal point of view, there are absolutely no requirements or restrictions on breed, size, or other specific type of dog. I find this to be an interesting dilemma that is undoubtedly headed for a collision with growing local interests on specific breed restrictions. Individuals with disabilities have a legal right with a federal base to be accompanied by their service dogs anywhere that serves the public. Federal statutes take precedent over state or local ones. So long as the dog meets the US Department of Justice definition of a service animal, it would seem unlikely to me that any state or local government will be allowed to dispute the definition or restrict access.

With those distinctions in mind, let's move on to the good stuff—what exactly are these dogs capable of doing and how can they help people?

---

[2] For further information on additional state-by-state legislation on service dogs, see the booklet "Legal Rights of Guide Dogs, Hearing Dogs and Service Dogs," published and sold by Assistance Dogs International. It contains information about the ADA, FAA, and HUD regulations as well as statutes from all 50 states and the District of Columbia. Ordering information is available at *www.assistancedogsinternational.com* or by calling 707-571-0427.

TASKS

In later chapters we'll undertake a more in-depth discussion of the tasks dogs can be trained to perform. But let's hit a few highlights now to establish the basis for our other topics. Service dogs can do such a variety of jobs it would require an encyclopedia to give a comprehensive list. The possibilities are as widely varied as are the disabilities of different people, so instead of trying to do a full list, let's look at a few of the most common types. In Chapter 7 we'll explore how the basics can be expanded.

Popular Favorites

In my experience, if I had to choose two tasks that were the most popular, most needed, and most frequently used, they would be (1) pulling a wheelchair and (2) fetching a cordless telephone.

Many people who have difficulty walking, or who spend much time in a wheelchair, have had the disagreeable and dangerous experience of falling. The fortunate are within shouting distance of someone who can help. The less fortunate may have a serious, even life-threatening, problem. The ability to have a cordless telephone delivered immediately to hand is a safety feature that often decides whether or not a disabled person is able to live alone.

Then the mobility issue: if you've never used a manual wheelchair, you might find it interesting to give it a try. Stop by your local grocery store or "mart" of whatever flavor and try out one of the courtesy chairs you see near the entrance. Put your feet up on the footrests and your hands on the wheels. Spend about thirty minutes rolling yourself around the store in simulated shopping. Now count the muscles in your arms and wrists and back—all those ones that you didn't know you had. Think about the college-bound student who has miles of campus to cover and doesn't want to have to be dependent on any else's schedule or help. Voila, the service dog.

I've been surprised over the years by how many folks will respond to this scenario by asking, "Why doesn't the person just get an electric chair?" Why, indeed. Let's set aside for a moment the fact that many of them cost as much as a car. They normally are heavy enough to require a mechanical lift (another expense) to load into a vehicle. Maintenance is an issue with any electronic device. And finally, far more simply, many people who use wheelchairs are under strong medical advice to use the manual chairs to maintain their upper body muscles. Yet when there is a question of long distance to be covered, the dog can be a huge saver of time and effort.

"Faster Than Anybody Else!"

"I'd prefer you not call it a disability," Mrs. Johnson told me sternly from her wheelchair. "It was an accident, but anyone can have an accident."

I hastily agreed and mended my terminology. Already in awe of this feisty 77-year-old lady, I was anxious to do anything to help. A stroke had resulted in the amputation of both of her legs. An extremely active, independent lifestyle changed abruptly. But the habits of a lifetime don't change overnight; merely forgetting she was in a wheelchair had already caused numerous falls. After two broken wrists, several less serious injuries, and an entire night spent on the floor beside her bed, Mrs. Johnson was willing to listen to her daughter's suggestion about a service dog—but she wasn't yet convinced. The jury was still out.

"Young lady," she said, fixing her clear blue eyes on me, "Everything takes more time now, and everything is much harder to do. From what you're saying, this dog sounds like a lot of trouble. I'm interested in help, not more work. Why would I want to do this?"

Needless to say, our training discussions over the following weeks were lively—but not nearly as lively as the phone call that came a couple months later from Mrs. Johnson's daughter.

"We have a problem!" The voice on the phone transmitted much frustration.

"Oh boy...what's wrong?" I was accustomed to such calls, but never quite accustomed to the corresponding assault of nerves. My mind could create 10 horror-scenarios per second of miscreant canines.

"Well," she said, "let me just tell you. You know we wanted this dog really for the main reason of him being able to get a phone for mother if she needed help."

"Yes, of course," I said. "If he's not doing well with that, we will get him straightened around. Be sure!"

"Oh, he's getting the phone just fine," came the response. "That's not a problem. He does it anytime she asks. The problem is this wheelchair business. Mother won't stay home. She's always going down the street to visit friends without letting me know. She will NOT stay with me when we shop. She's goes off on her own, to other stores even. What's worse, the dog moves her chair so fast, I can't catch up!"

I ran a quick mental review to assure myself that we were, indeed, discussing a mother, not a child. Besides which, I knew from many weeks of training that Mrs. Johnson's mental capacities were sharper than my own. "Is she having any problem with the dog behaving or helping her?"

"No, of course not," fumed the frustrated daughter. "But how can I make this dog stay with me? Obviously Mother is not going to listen."

An interesting conversation followed which was highly unsatisfactory to the daughter, but probably just the reverse for Mrs. Johnson. As I hung up the telephone, I thought back to the enormous smile that broke out on the elderly lady's face on the day she was finally mastering the art of dog-pulling-wheelchair. Many hours of practice were paying off handsomely.

"Why, I can get there faster than anybody else!" she said, absolutely beaming. "Good boy, Chester. Let's go."

As I watched them zip off down the busy park sidewalk, I retired to a nearby bench to watch and savor the moment. In service dog work, this is the peak of the crest—a surge of enormous satisfaction cannot be explained to one who's never done it. As I watched Mrs. Johnson and Chester grow tiny in the distance, I felt no concern, but a quiet exhilaration. She didn't need my help anymore—she had her dog. A life renewed. Independence regained.

More Variety

Moving on to other tasks: dogs can fetch objects indicated by pointing (with a hand or with a laser pointer). They can carry items in their mouth or their backpacks. They can open doors—household, mall, and refrigerator. They can pull your socks off and your bed covers up. Dogs can deposit items in the trash, the washing machine, the kitchen sink, and your tote bag. They can fetch a telephone when it rings—or find it when it doesn't. Dogs can turn on a light, an appliance, an alarm system, or anything else with an appropriate switch or button. They can learn the difference between the TV remote and your car keys—and probably find either faster than you can. The list is nearly endless.

Seizures or blackouts can be aided to some degree by a dog who is trained to make certain responses. We'll discuss this more in Chapter 7, but a consistent pattern to a seizure disorder allows a dog to be trained to summon help or provide assistance in specific ways.

People with limited mobility but who are able to walk face just as many dilemmas in their varied situations as those using wheelchairs. Dogs can help with balance. Again, they can carry items in their mouths or in backpacks. If getting up from a chair is a major task for you, the dog can still get you that darned phone faster than you can—or before it stops ringing. Some people with balance trouble, bone or joint impairment, or spinal problems can walk fairly well—but dropping something on the floor means it might as well be three states away. A dog's backpack—or retrieve—puts needed items back into reach.

Help With Mental Health

Dogs who assist with psychiatric disabilities have jobs that are somewhat harder to quantify and explain, but in certain cases very legitimate. Post Traumatic Stress Disorder (PTSD) is a good example. This disability can manifest itself in a variety of ways. What behavior is helpful from a dog depends on the person's particular situation. A dog can provide a valuable focus point or initiate a certain interaction at the onset of symptoms. Such a thing could be as simple as pressure on a leg or persistent nudging in response to certain behaviors. Again, depending on a person's particular circumstances, such assistance from a dog may provide a break in the cycle that would otherwise feed on itself and grow.[3]

Social Help

For some people, the psychological benefits of having an assistance dog are hugely important. Some people find the dogs helpful in a social sense—the dogs are not only a constant companion but an incredible conversation piece! (One of my clients from recent years referred to his assistance dog as "the chick magnet.") On the other hand, I've also met plenty of people who are offended by the concept and consider that any such idea would equal using the dog as a social crutch. From a personal point of view, I don't happen to agree, since my own animals are such an major part of my life that it's difficult to maintain friendships with those who don't like dogs. But to twist an old phrase: that's personal, not business.

Differing opinions on service dogs providing social help provide an excellent illustration of the point about individuality. *Service dogs serve different purposes for different people!* The differences are practical, mental, emotional, logistical. You can no more restrict types of assistance with rigid definitions than you can the K–12 education of children. What works in some cases simply does not work in others. One person's needs are entirely

---

[3] The web site of the International Association of Assistance Dog Partners (IAADP) contains a superb article by Joan Froling on the potential benefits of using service dogs to give assistance with issues of mental health. See "Service Dog Tasks for Psychiatric Disabilities," at *www.iaadp.org/psd_tasks.html.*

different from another's. In fact, even one person with one disability—such as Multiple Sclerosis—likely has varying needs from month to month or even day to day.

Combinations

In recent years several training schools have begun training what they refer to as "combination" dogs, who are both assistance dogs and guide dogs. This is a highly complex form of training that is not yet widespread. The results are wonderful, but certainly at the very highest end of the training spectrum for complexity and demands on both trainer and owner.

No Protection

One word of caution about what an assistance dog is not. They are *not* protection dogs. While it is true that the mere presence of the dog might provide some additional security for a handler, the dog's function is *not* about protection. The legal basis for public accommodation does not include protection. The Americans with Disabilities Act does refer to service dogs performing "minimal protection and rescue work"[4] but this statement does not refer to aggressiveness toward other people. It refers to protecting a person's health or safety from the disabling condition itself, such as summoning help, preventing falls, or making certain responses during blackouts or seizures. In fact, the US Department of Justice specifically provides businesses or public services the right to exclude any service dog displaying aggressive behavior to other people.[5] Any individual's desire to have a personal protection dog is absolutely no grounds for getting a service dog. The only

---

[4] Code of Federal Regulations: 28CFR36.104 [page 548]. The CFR is available online at *www.findlaw.com/casecode/cfr.html* or at *www.legal.gsa.gov*.
[5] "Commonly Asked Questions About Service Animals in Places of Business, US Department of Justice," *www.usdoj.gov/crt/ada/qasrvc.htm*, or call 1-800-514-0301 and ask for Fax #3204.

legitimate basis for using a service dog in public is a disability that is helped by the dog's assistance.

IN CONCLUSION

So if you are the person with a disability and something in your life needs help being fetched, moved, dragged, pulled, located, alerted, balanced, carried, pushed, nudged, touched, guided, or pressed…a dog might be a good solution for you.

SUGGESTED READING

The Delta Society maintains an online library, which contains a large number of extremely helpful resources and articles, both basic and specific, about service dogs, their jobs, and interaction with today's culture and issues. You can visit this collection of articles at *www.deltasociety.org/nsdc/sdresources.htm*.

Chapter 3:

Dogs Are Not Furry People

Service dogs are a matter for careful contemplation before any decisions are made; they are not always the best practical solution for people with disabilities. Kind (but often unrealistic) attempts by publishers and producers to give recognition and respect to the dogs and people have far too often presented an overly rosy view of service work. Before we even begin considering the complexities of training, prospective owners of service dogs should probably consider far more basic issues. At the heart of the discussion is something that seems to be a common, but much believed fallacy: a trained dog is the equivalent of a vending machine. The dog is "trained," right? So speaking a certain sound unfailingly nets you a certain result, right? Not hardly! Just as legendary coach Vince Lombardi once re-centered his football team on the basics ("Gentlemen, this is a football."), I would like to draw attention to a rather obvious, but often-overlooked little fact: folks, we're dealing with a dog.

CHAPTER 3: DOGS ARE NOT FURRY PEOPLE

SOCIAL WORRIES

Obvious, yes. But easily forgotten. Because it is a dog, it also sheds, excretes, urinates, pants, drools, vomits, scratches, chews on things for fun, and does not use breath mints. Contrary to many of our cultural norms these days, a dog is not a small furry human. Rarely have I read a truer statement than the closing comment from Stephen Budiansky's book, *The Truth About Dogs,* "If dogs truly were human, they would be jerks. As dogs, they are wonderful."[1] Left to his own devices and inclinations, almost any dog trotting down a public sidewalk will sniff people in the groin, eat grass and throw it up, consume trash or feces, roll in a cadaver, and urinate every 24 inches. This is normal canine culture, part of the basic nature of a dog. If any human tried such things, he'd shortly be in a psychiatric facility, if not in jail.

Now, hold on a moment! Before I discourage you completely from the service dog idea—please understand this is not my intent. For those willing to work hard and think in realistic terms, a service dog relationship will probably be one of the most rewarding efforts you've ever undertaken. But it would be unfair to present it as a sort of "drive-through" solution…as though you one day meet your dog, learn his name, and trot blissfully into the sunset to live happily ever after. As with any relationship (canine or human!), you'll have a lot of learning to do—along with adjusting and accepting.

Fate's Role

I remember getting this lecture as a novice, newly entered in the apprentice trainer program. I also remember *remembering* this lecture a few months later as I scrambled about the concrete floor in a Lowe's Home Improvement Warehouse, frantically grabbing

---

[1] Stephen Budiansky, *The Truth About Dogs*. New York: Penguin Books, 2001.

feces from the floor, wadding it up in receipts and old Kleenex, and stuffing it into my purse. The Labrador on the other end of the leash was only a trainee—and this was the very first time we'd entered a store. A bowel movement had not been in my plan, and certainly not in the store management's plan, but Brewster seemed to think otherwise. That episode was the first time it really sank into my head that all the training in the world wouldn't help if the dog just absolutely had to go and just…well, DID. No, it's not anywhere near common, especially with a finished dog. But it's a risk you are going to take, and no trainer, no veterinarian, no behaviorist can ever absolutely guarantee you it's not going to happen. In fact, even during the time I was working on this book, I read a news clip on the CNN web site about a guide dog who did the same thing—on the court at a halftime show during an NBA game in Orlando!

Aside from such extreme problems, other issues can be more, or less, obvious. The degree and variety of potential embarrassment is pretty unlimited. For many people, service dogs are a boon they wouldn't trade for anything. But it's worthy of note how many people run screaming to their trainers within hours of their first solo venture. "I can't believe he [fill in public atrocity here]!!!"

Great Potential

Again, I have no intentions of trying to discourage you from considering a service dog. I only want you to think ahead to the potential drawbacks of what you are signing up for. Doesn't everything in life have advantages and disadvantages? It's fair and reasonable to spend adequate time considering both. A service dog could magnify the quality of your life in more ways than I know how to tell you. But don't kid yourself that it's easy, or even on the lower side of hard. A successful handler/service dog team working together represents an enormous amount of effort and understanding. Before you make any decision, I hope you will look beyond the romantic stories that never mention the gritty details. Ask lots of questions. Make an informed decision. Understand what you're signing up for. If your first question is "How can I get a dog that never sheds?" you might want to slow down and consider other options. On the other hand, you might discover the enhancement a dog brings to your life is of far more value than a little dog hair on the furniture.

"She Likes to Play Outside"

The perfectly-groomed young woman surveyed the array of paw prints on her glistening kitchen floor. Distaste radiated from her expression. "What am I supposed to do about the mud?"

This was not an auspicious beginning. We'd barely made it in the door—and had almost had to swim through the driving rainstorm to get that far. It was always fun to anticipate a client's excitement about the new dog's much-awaited arrival, but this time other concerns seemed greater.

"She knows a command of 'wait,'" I told her. "I'd recommend you stop her just inside the door and towel her off."

"Every time she goes outside?" Jenny wasn't impressed with this concept. "Won't that be several times a day? Can't she learn to wipe her feet?"

Stifling a sigh, I suggested we delay the housecleaning agenda for a just a bit and work on more basic concepts at the start. It was a long process, but the relationship did become functional. How much it would grow, I could not possibly have predicted!

Six months later it was time to do a follow-up visit on Jenny and Amber. Bracing myself for the normal dissection of technique for hygiene and house decor, I took a deep breath and rang the doorbell. A moment later I heard the patter of trotting paws and Amber pulled the door lever. I was glad to see her—otherwise I might have thought I was in the wrong residence.

Wasn't this floor white? I thought in amazement. No longer. A nearly uniform coating of red South Carolina clay was spread throughout the kitchen. Floor. Cupboards. Refrigerator. Walls. Applying a brick-colored chair rail at 32 inches would have seemed appropriate.

CHAPTER 3: DOGS ARE NOT FURRY PEOPLE

"Hi!" The enthusiastic response came from the hallway. Jenny couldn't even wait to get all the way into the room before beginning her recitation of Amber's virtues. "Did I tell you that we went to the opera last week? I was so afraid she would whine or howl about the music, but she was just perfect!"

Finally I could actually see the owner of the voice as she wheeled into the kitchen.

"And she got her picture on the 'staff directory' board at work. My boss says she deserves recognition as much as anyone else who works there."

Much later, when there was pause enough to get into a training discussion, I asked how the towel-against-mud campaign was progressing. The answer came with a completely blank look.

"Towels?" Jenny asked? "What for? Oh! You mean because of the mud." She waved her hand dismissively. "I got tired of towels. Now I just let her in the kitchen and close the door until she's dried off. I park the car in front and when we go out, we leave by the front door and stay on the sidewalk."

"Great," I said. "Do you need any help getting her to go to the bathroom on leash? Or, ummm…anything I could do to simplify the drying-off process …or…." I was running out of words. I didn't want to comment on the obvious to this woman who had always maintained her own version of house beautiful. What was this dog doing…going out and BATHING in mud?

"No, not really," Jenny responded. She likes to play outside, so I'd rather do it this way. She's easier to clean off when she's dry. This works okay."

There was nothing more for me to say. The dog was functional and safe. The owner was thrilled. Never mind that the amount of mud in the kitchen was something even I would have had trouble tolerating. It was none of my business. How much more so came home to me about a year later when I approached the same kitchen door. A small cross-stitched sign now hung on the exterior—a version of a poster I'd seen for sale in various dog catalogs: "This house is maintained for the comfort and safety of my dog. If you don't like that, please go away."

Indeed.

Common Problems

If dogs are new to you, go to the pet section of almost any bookstore for a good education in the basics. Take note of the long shelves full of books about training, about coping, about choosing the right dog, and about how to incorporate him into your home. *Every single one of these issues applies to you.* The difference is that for you, every issue is an even larger one than what others face with their pets. Most people who read those books are merely trying to manage the dog in their home, the park, the car, at the veterinarian's office, and perhaps a friend's home now and then.

You, as a prospective service dog owner, are going to have to manage the exact same behaviors everywhere you go—in front of a large, never-ending (and pretty critical) audience commonly referred to as "the public." Because a dog is legally a service animal doesn't make the rest of the canine issues go away. The dog hasn't studied the law. Even a completely functional, well-trained service dog can often run into a problem situation because other people simply do not understand dogs.

Murphy's Law

Some years ago I had a client call me in near hysteria. Though this man, Andy, was calling from his own home, his voice was an urgent whisper. "I think the police are looking for me."

What?! I thought in alarm. Andy's dog, Casper, was an extremely sociable Golden Retriever. It was hard to imagine him biting someone. What else would call for the police?

As events unfolded, I realized that Casper was actually being a little too sociable. We'd always had trouble communicating with Casper that it really wasn't necessary to bathe people in order to communicate good will. Casper didn't just "lick." He put his heart and soul into it.

The day that the above-mentioned phone call took place, it was summertime in the south. Many people were wearing shorts and other cool clothing. Casper was quite well known for a very sloppy lick on the nearest anatomical part of anyone within reach.

What Andy learned that day was to watch for people he hadn't even known were "in reach." He and Casper had been shopping in a warehouse-type grocery store. As they passed an employee (who was wearing shorts and standing a step or two up on a short ladder), Casper turned his head and gave the woman a juicy slurp on the back of the knee without even breaking stride. The woman yelped, fell off the ladder, then looked up to see a large man and dog moving away. For reasons we never quite understood, there was no convincing her that the dog, not the man, had made the move. Failing to gain his point with the store manager, Andy fled and raced to a phone. Program personnel implemented a good bit of soothing public relations during the rest of that day. Casper returned to a special boot camp for a couple weeks to convince him that the licking had to tone down. Andy learned to be very alert.

Though this is truly a once-in-a-lifetime scenario, I relate it here as proof that no one can really ever predict the full variety of factors you'll face in public over the years of a dog's working life. Service dogs are thinking, breathing, sensate animals, not automatons. If you don't like dogs, don't like their personalities, their quirks, and their habits, don't fool yourself by thinking that a service dog will be any more attractive to you than any other dog. Make your decision on that basis and expect reality, not miracles.

SPECIFIC CONSIDERATIONS

On the more technical side, a list of specific questions to consider will help you understand more completely the pros and cons for your situation. Before you proceed, do yourself the favor of providing written answers to the questions below (include input from your health professionals where applicable).

Y/N   Is anyone in your household allergic to dogs?

Y/N   Does your budget allow for the feeding and care of a dog? This issue includes parasite control and extra cleaning needed in your home. Depending on where you live and the size of your dog, this can easily total around $1,000 per year. A single major illness for your dog could add hundreds of dollars to that figure.

Y/N   Does your schedule—whether at home or at work—allow for the time necessary to care for the dog? This includes time for grooming, bathing (or transporting him for someone else to perform these jobs), exercise, on-going training, and several-times-per-day potty breaks.

Y/N   Are you physically able to care for the dog if he were to become ill?

Y/N   Do you have access to someone who could care for the dog, or the finances to board him, in an emergency or if you were to become ill enough for hospitalization or otherwise unable to care for him?

Y/N   Could anything about your disability be worsened or aggravated by the use of a service dog? (For example, repetitive stress complications from holding a dog's harness as he pulls your wheelchair?)

Y/N   Is everyone in your household in agreement that a service dog is a good plan and willing to do his part? One uncooperative person in a household can be enough to derail almost any otherwise successful effort.

Y/N   What other animals are in your home and can they be managed in such a way as not to pose any threat to the physical well-being or the working effectiveness of your service dog?

Y/N   If you have no suitable trainer or program nearby, are you able and willing to travel, probably more than once, to complete the application and training process? This may involve several weeks at a time away from home.

Y/N   Are your living conditions and related employment, or other income source, stable enough that a move out of your immediate area is unlikely? You could have the perfect trainer nearby, but it might not be a lot of help if circumstances force a move three states away, perhaps even before the initial training process is complete.

Y/N   Do you have practical access to veterinary care, either your own transportation or public transportation that will put you within reasonable reach of your vet's office? Remember that if your dog is ill in a way that would soil his surroundings, normal means of transportation (even a close friend) may be problematic.

Y/N   Do you have a backup plan available for necessary tasks which the service dog might not be able to perform if he was ill?

Y/N   Does your job or lifestyle involve international travel? Keep in mind that not all countries allow public access for service animals.

CHAPTER 3: DOGS ARE NOT FURRY PEOPLE

Y/N   If your regular means of transportation is a personal vehicle, is it large enough to accommodate the addition of a dog riding with you? Are you willing to tolerate muddy pawprints on upholstery and carpet? Rain, snow, and mud in public places will make mess inevitable.

Y/N   Do you have any neighbors who are antagonistic to dogs? If so, do you have a means of providing exercise and relief for your dog that will minimize his contact with the neighbors?

Y/N   Are your relatives and close friends in favor of you acquiring a service dog? If there are negative reactions, how important will this be to you in terms of family gatherings, holidays, and so on? Remember that the law does not require individuals to allow service animals in private homes—only in places that serve the general public.

Y/N   In light of the fact that the average service dog's working life is 8–10 years, maximum (though smaller dogs are generally longer-lived), is the expenditure of effort, time, and funds worth that limited length of time to you? For most people, a service dog is not a life-long solution and, even if remarkably effective, will need to be replaced in time.

Chapter 4:

Certification

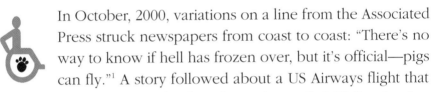
In October, 2000, variations on a line from the Associated Press struck newspapers from coast to coast: "There's no way to know if hell has frozen over, but it's official—pigs can fly."[1] A story followed about a US Airways flight that contained a 300-lb pig in the first class cabin. Why? Well...simple. Its owner showed up to travel and told airline personnel that the pig was a service animal. US Airways received an enormous amount of criticism following the incident. News reports varied considerably. Depending on whose account you choose to believe, passengers were particularly non-understanding when the pig panicked and ran through the plane, tried to enter the cockpit, defecated, then was contained in (or possibly refused to leave?) the galley, during approach and landing in Seattle.

"How ridiculous," you say. Oh really? Mull over the rocky truth that the US Airways staff acted correctly according to legal principle. They did exactly what they would have been expected to do according to the ADA and related guidelines from the

---

[1] For various accounts, see *seattlepi.nwsource.com/local/pigs281.shtml* and *www.washingtonpost.com/wp_srv/aponline/20001027/aponline212651_000.htm*.

Federal Aviation Administration. Shortly after the incident, the FAA cleared US Airways of any incorrect action.[2] If they had refused to accommodate the pig, the owner might very well have sued them for non-accommodation. Federal rules require that airlines allow a service animal to travel in the cabin with its disabled owner. The law does not say that a service animal cannot be a pig. Though airline personnel are allowed to ask for an example of how the animal assists the individual, the law does not allow specific questioning about the person's disability itself. The law does not require certification or documentation to validate an animal (even a pig) as a service animal.

If that seems a little hard to stretch your brain around, be sure you're not alone. Certification is one of the most commonly misunderstood concepts about service dogs. I could not possibly count contacts I've received in which people ask me, "I have someone to train a service dog, but how do I get it certified?" This question is asked with all honorable intent—the same as one might very logically ask, "Okay, I've finished Driver's Education, how do I get a license?" When the truth is there is *no* standardized "license," or "certification" for service animals.

How can that be possible, you're thinking. (I heard you!) All you have to do is open the phone book to read about "certified" trainers. You see features and articles about "certified" dogs? Obviously certification exists…right? Yes, it does. But you need to understand what the term really means and separate it from the concept of legality.

LEGAL SERVICE ANIMALS

Fine then…what makes a service dog legal? Fair question. The right to use service animals in places that serve the public is granted to

---

[2] "Airline was right to let pig fly, FAA says," *www.CNN.com*, November 29, 2000.

individuals with disabilities by the Americans with Disabilities Act of 1990 (Public Law 101-336). This act was passed to ensure a nondiscriminatory basis for people with disabilities to function in American society. The protection, therefore, afforded to service dogs through the ADA, *belongs to the disabled person, not to the dog*. With that distinction in mind, it becomes easier to understand that any claims of certification, either of a dog or of a trainer, have their basis in efforts toward quality control, marketing, and/or identification of ownership and liability. Certification has nothing to do with whether or not the dog is legal.

DEFINITION FROM U.S. DEPARTMENT OF JUSTICE

The following excerpt is from the Department of Justice's publication, "Commonly Asked Questions About Service Animals in Places of Business."[3]

Q: What is a service animal?

A: The ADA defines a service animal as any guide dog, signal dog, or other animal individually trained to provide assistance to an individual with a disability. If they meet this definition, animals are considered service animals under the ADA regardless of whether they have been licensed or certified by a state or local government.

Q: How can I tell if an animal is really a service animal and not just a pet?

A: Some, but not all, service animals wear special collars and harnesses. Some, but not all, are licensed or certified and have identification papers. If you are not certain that an animal is a

---

[3] This entire document can be viewed on the web site of the US Department of Justice, at *www.usdoj.gov/crt/ada/qasrvc.htm*, or you can call 1-800-514-0301 and ask for information about Fax #3204.

service animal, you may ask the person who has the animal if it is a service animal required because of a disability. However, an individual who is going to a restaurant or theater is not likely to be carrying documentation of his or her medical condition or disability. Therefore, such documentation generally may not be required as a condition for providing service to an individual accompanied by a service animal. Although a number of states have programs to certify service animals, you may not insist on proof of state certification before permitting the service animal to accompany the person with a disability.

The legal definition of a service dog, and/or its owner's right to be accompanied by the dog in public places, does not currently contain any reference to the presence or absence of certification.[4]

WHAT IS CERTIFICATION?

Certified Dogs

In short, certification normally represents an agreement—usually a written contract—between a trainer and a client, concerning a specific animal. Many service dog training agencies provide a photo identification card, much like a driver's license, that represents the contract, indicating the owner, the trainer, and the certification date. The normal, appropriate implication would be that the dog has had specific training for the job, has passed a minimum performance test, and has been correctly incorporated

---

[4] Code of Federal Regulations: 28CFR36.104 [page 548], "Service animal means any guide dog, signal dog, or other animal individually trained to do work or perform tasks for the benefit of an individual with a disability, including, but not limited to, guiding individuals with impaired vision, alerting individuals with impaired hearing to intruders or sounds, providing minimal protection or rescue work, pulling a wheelchair, or fetching dropped items." You can view the CFR online at *www.findlaw.com/casecode/cfr.html* or *www.legal.gsa.gov*.

into the working environment with the owner. Many such certifications expire and must be renewed on a regular basis. Normally, programs that use certifications encourage or require the owner to display the certification tag on the dog's collar or harness while in public. While assistance dogs are legally the responsibility of their owner, any attorney worth the term can assure you that in the event of a lawsuit, an issuer of a certification tag is taking a certain amount of *de facto* responsibility for the conduct of that dog.

"Isn't There Something Official?"

"I know getting angry doesn't help, but it's awfully hard not to. This is the second time it's happened. I cannot afford this in terms of time or money." The man on the phone was winding up his third story of our conversation. We hadn't met, but I felt we were getting rapidly acquainted. Steve had called to ask if there wasn't some way he could complete a curriculum or review or test through Dogs for Disabled and obtain a "legal certification." He was tired of being challenged about his service dog. I had already explained that what he asked wasn't possible. But listening to his stories made me wish, once again, that legal circumstances were different.

With the acquisition of his privately-trained service dog, Steve had been able to re-start the sales business that had been interrupted years before by his auto accident. He was still within the first year of operation, and struggling to meet each expense. The nature of the work called for much public interaction; he and Brady, his Lab, were in and out of various businesses all day, almost every day. The frequent contact was resulting in many challenges from people who didn't understand about service dogs. The worst problem was that twice now the resulting delays had caused him to miss flight reservations—the last one when he had been detained by a building's security guard while the police were called.

"This is a very busy job and requires that I keep a very tight schedule, "Steve went on, now just blowing off steam. "It's because I HAVE this dog that I'm able to work, so now I'm working and on the go all day. Sometimes I run into people half a dozen times a day who want to argue a no-dogs rule. You know, I understand that sometimes people just don't know. Most advocacy groups say you should be willing to spend time helping people understand. But I cannot possibly educate the whole world, and I can't spend more time 'educating' than working. Don't others have some responsibility too? Besides that, you know, it's really none of their darned business."

The frustration I felt during the conversation was not new, but no less sharp for the repetition. No, it wasn't any of their darned business. But the year was 1995, and far fewer people were familiar with service dogs than today. Even now, with increased awareness, much of the problem remains.

"Isn't there something?" Steve persisted "Something official? Something that even the least-informed illiterate would recognize and stop wasting my time?"

Ten years later my answer to these people is still the same. No, there isn't anything official. I always try to help them put together an ID card for their dog, showing its photo and quoting the Department of Justice's policy about service animals. But as both a trainer and a user of service dogs I am sympathetic to the plight. The frustration, and sometimes embarrassment, of being singled out and challenged can be significant. In Steve's case, not to mention expensive—a double-whammy of missed flights cost him well over a thousand dollars.

Certified Trainers

Of course, now and then you will also encounter the term "certified trainer." Very likely you'll do so even as you begin shopping for an assistance dog! Most often, trainer certification represents a graduation certificate—a stamp of approval—from a particular school or institution. (Except for specific states who require licensing for certain types of service training, such as guide dogs.) The resulting amount of training proficiency depends both on the instruction and on the skill and experience of the trainer. Most such schools have courses in generalized dog training. A few have curriculum specifically designed for the training of assistance dogs.

The quality of the certification, then, depends both on the individual trainer and also on the quality of the instruction. Given the widely separated schools of thought among trainers (much of it diametrically opposed), any trainer's claim of certification actually means very little until one understands what is behind the term and through what process it was obtained. There is no federal standardization of such processes, and rarely even at the state level, such as one would expect for teachers or nurses. One certified trainer might actually have had many years of classroom instruction, combined with directed apprenticeship and be extremely capable of helping almost any client. Another might have completed the training protocol entirely by correspondence course. Anyone looking to verify the abilities of an assistance dog trainer will need to look farther than the term itself. We'll talk more about how to judge the quality of training in later chapters.

WHAT IS CERTIFICATION NOT?

Certification Is Not a Quality Guarantee

You could make a huge mistake in your service dog research by assuming certification is a fool-proof guarantee. Going back to the educational parallels, determining the value of certification is much like choosing a college. If a college tells you it is accredited, your first question will very likely be…"By whom?" Other questions would be "Since when?" "According to what criteria?" and "Where can I meet some graduates for their opinions on the matter?" And those are pretty much the same questions anyone should ask when shopping for assistance dogs.

Certification is essentially a question of "accreditation," or approval by a party outside the immediate working relationship. It can give you lots more information. It can spread around the burden of responsibility for results. *But don't mistake certification for a guarantee of quality,* any more than you should confuse certification with legality. The ability of a trainer to effectively train an assistance dog cannot be correctly measured by only the presence or absence of certification.

Certification Is Not a Shortcut

When I first became involved with service dog training, one of the most startling aspects I had to learn to deal with were phone calls from people asking me to certify their pet as an assistance dog—though no disability was involved. Or perhaps someone in the family actually had a disability, but the dog was not trained to assist. Evidently the owners considered the presence of the disability to be close enough. A well-worn excuse for such misrepresentation is so a family can keep the dog in housing that has is a no-pets policy. Unbelievable? Yes. Common? Also yes.

Very similar are the questions from people who want to take Rover on the family vacation and desire assistance dog certification so he can fly in the cabin of the plane with them or stay at a no-pets resort. "But I've seen other people flying with dogs!" Indeed, they probably have. Possibly both legitimate ones and otherwise. Unfortunately, our society contains plenty of people willing to lie on this level; to deny that is naive. Such deception is both incredibly unfair and incredibly dangerous. No respectable service dog trainer will entertain such an idea under any circumstances. Any person who would do so would be exposing himself to many kinds of civil litigation and even possible criminal penalties.

PRACTICAL CONSIDERATIONS

Some years ago, due to health complications, I spent a stretch of time as a service dog user, as well as a trainer. Somewhere in the middle of that very educational year I had to take a series of interstate trips involving a variety of airlines. Time after time, I wearily repeated answers to the (correct) questions asked by airline personnel at ticket counters. "I cannot walk without the dog's help." (It is FAA policy that they ask for an example of how the dog helps its owner.) Uncounted times I explained to fellow passengers, passers-by, and others that no I was not blind and the dog was not guiding me. "Yes, the dog is allowed to travel in the cabin with me. No, she will not bite you. No, you cannot pet her." But all these issues were expected.

What I certainly had not expected to hear were stories from flight attendants about service animals who growled or snapped at passengers and urinated on walls. I heard from airport personnel about dogs who were too terrified to ride on the transportation carts and who wouldn't stop barking. I listened to four different stories from fellow travelers, told in conspiratorial confidence, about how they "did the same thing. Why, I just told them this was my service dog and flew all the way to Peoria." Most unbelievably, I also had a well-recognized dog trainer remark, "Wow, I sure want to get one of those harnesses. It's a too cool way to get around! The only thing anybody ever says to you is, 'what a beautiful dog!'"

The temptation is enormous to get off topic here about my personal thoughts about a need for means of service animal validation and quality standards. But we'll save that for later except to say that I believe one is needed, and I believe that sooner or later, such a system will happen in the United States. The mere thought of having such a system is one of the most controversial and hotly-contested pieces of turf around. In some circles the concept is nearly enough to start a fist fight. However, most readers of this book have far more immediate and pressing needs than solving such a broad controversy. What is real? And what is here and now? For the purpose of discerning what *you* need, and where to get it, this issue distills to a few specifics you should keep in mind.

Certification is Valuable

Certification may not be necessary for you to use a service dog in public, but keeping some documentation of the law on hand might save a lot of frustration. Hardly a week goes by that I do not hear yet another story from an assistance dog owner that he or she was challenged, embarrassed, or asked to leave a particular place. Very often because they "didn't have an ID" proving the dog was an assistance dog. While it's very true the law does not say you must have one, you can be sure that having one can simplify and shorten many excursions—not to mention deflecting the intrusive questions you might not want to have to answer anyway. You can find an excellent printable copy of a suitable document, courtesy of the Delta Society, at *www.deltasociety.org/nsdc/dsb010.htm*.

Certification is Common

Programs and trainers in the service dog world have, in recent years, begun a process of self-regulating, primarily through Assistance Dogs International, a non-profit group dedicated to the standardization and quality enhancement of assistance dogs nationwide. Membership is voluntary, requires dues and pledged adherence to minimum standards, as well as to the code of ethics. I believe the concept is excellent, and the intentions good. The practical aspects still need much refinement, but, as in most reputable organizations, that will happen as a natural result of growth and maturity in the years ahead. Most organizations affiliated with ADI use some sort of contractual certification arrangement with their clients. Somewhere in the future, I believe the type of standardization they are trying to achieve will be required by federal law.

EVALUATING CERTIFICATION

Meanwhile, if you are screening a trainer or a program for competency and reliability, here are a few suggestions to get you started.

Affiliation with Assistance Dogs International

Assistance Dogs International,[5] a non-profit organization established by voluntary cooperation of various programs, is dedicated to establishing standards and increasing excellence in the service dog world. Much can be learned by determining if a trainer or program is affiliated with Assistance Dogs International (ADI), as well as their reasons for affiliating—or not. If you ask, "Is your training group affiliated with ADI?" and the answer is "Who?", be wary. If the answer is yes, that's probably a pretty good start. If the answer is "no," but they are familiar with the organization, the criterion, and have a well-considered reason for their choice not to affiliate, that's still probably a pretty good start. It's possible that only one or two considerations, differences of training methodology, or other purely logistical problems prevent a trainer or group from making an official association. In this instance, a good follow-up question is whether or not a trainer uses a minimum performance test for its dogs that is at least equivalent to the ADI's Minimum Performance Test.[6] If the answer is "yes," ask to see the written version.

Observation

Ask the trainer or program to allow you to observe the dog and the trainer completing the Minimum Performance Test, as discussed

---

[5] Assistance Dogs International maintains an extensive and extremely helpful web site at www.assistancedogsinternational.com/. Their material provides good research about what to expect of a service dog training program.

[6] ADI's suggested minimum standard for a finished dog's performance in public is available at www.assistancedogsinternational.com/publicaccess.html.

above, or at least a videotape thereof. It's reasonable to expect you'll have some challenges when you start working the dog yourself—but don't complicate it by starting with an incompletely trained dog. See proof.

Alternatives

If you are considering a private trainer, or a group without an established Minimum Performance Test, I recommend your contract require the dog—*at least*—obtain a title of Companion Dog through the obedience trials of the American Kennel Club[7] or the United Kennel Club,[8] or obtain a title of Begleithund (BH, or "Companion Dog"), available through several organizations, including through the Working Dog Association[9] and the United Schutzhund Clubs of America.[10] The latter two organizations allow mixed-breed dogs to test for the BH at their events.

 Back up for a moment: given the wide variety of situations for which assistance dogs are trained, it would be impossible to standardize a test for specific assistance tasks—and perhaps useless—because many of the situations these dogs alleviate or assist with cannot be recreated at will. Furthermore, knowledge of some tasks an assistance dog performs for a person with a disability can easily violate privacy. This is not the business of the general public, nor even of a canine performance evaluator. But what is? If a dog is going to be accommodated in a public place, what is reasonable to expect that others in public should be able to count on? *Safety!* And, to a lesser extent, non-disruptive behavior. A Minimum Performance Test addresses these issues

---

[7] American Kennel Club, 5580 Centerview Drive, Raleigh, NC 27606. 919-233-9767.
[8] United Kennel Club, 100 East Kilgore Road, Kalamazoo, MI 49002. 269-343-9020.
[9] Working Dog Association, 1699 N. Jungle Den Rd. #45, Astor FL 32102. 386-749-4574.
[10] United Schutzhund Clubs of America, 3810 Paule Ave.St. Louis, MO 63125. 314-638-9686.

well—a Companion Dog title or a Begleithund test addresses at least the basics.

Any service dog worth the term should be able easily to pass the requirements for either the CD or the BH. Neither comes close to addressing all the issues suggested in the recommended Minimum Performance Test advocated by ADI. However, successful completion of any of these criteria requires a dog to demonstrate reasonable obedience on and off leash. The dog would have to show general control and good temperament, as well as lack of aggression to people and/or to other dogs even when not restrained by the handler. Additionally, the trainer is exhibiting willingness to subject the dog to professional, third-party evaluation.

If a private trainer you're considering can't prove the dog on at least this basis, I believe you would be better off to spend your money and time elsewhere. Children, the elderly, and, yes, even many with disabilities, are exhibiting their dogs for Companion Dog titles nearly every weekend of the year—and most of them are doing it just purely for fun. I have absolutely no reservation about saying that any dog who cannot easily pass these well-known tests has no business in public as a working dog.

PERSONAL RESPONSIBILITY

Please hear me, readers. Certification may not be an actual, specific legal requirement. But don't fool yourself: in the absence of a national certification requirement, the question of legality does not simply go away. The operative question is actually: "who is validating the presence of the dog?" Since certification is not required, the answer is "you are!" You are the legally responsible party. When and how to take a service dog in public is ultimately your own decision and the consequences, be they good or bad, will stop at your door. Therefore, this is not a place to allow good public relations with your trainer to preempt common sense.

The law states that a service dog must be specifically trained to assist with a particular disability. The burden of certainty is on you. Certainty for training. Certainty for safety. Be sure. Ultimately, you are the responsible party. Protect those around you. Protect yourself. Protect your dog. Deal in proof, not speculation. I believe that a standard of accountability is not a matter to be feared and shunned, but to be embraced and welcomed as proof of effectiveness. Essentially, at this time the law gives *you* control of that standard. Use it wisely.

Chapter 5:
Understanding & Evaluating Training Methods

"The only thing two dog trainers can agree on is what a third dog trainer is doing wrong." That rather cynical statement is an old joke in the dog world, but it's both frustrating and accurate. The endless differences of opinion about training methods can be viewed by a quick look at the pet section of almost any bookstore. Most trainers lay claim to a superior method, yet a casual scan through several books will probably show you very different advice. Most phone books carry a wide array of ads from local trainers—almost every one of them bristling with "qualifications, award-winning backgrounds, and national recognition." Service dog owners face all the same issues as regular dog owners—plus a lot more. Therefore, regardless that the different training methods were not developed specifically for service dogs, a whole lot of typical training factors in anyway.

How should a client choose a trainer or a program? How can one evaluate competence? Can quality be accurately anticipated? Anyone who wants to trust his functional safety to the behavior of a dog needs more than opinion or a sales pitch. For that matter, so does a sponsor who is being asked to contribute multiple thousands of dollars in support. Such folks need a definite measure for effectiveness of training. Furthermore, that measure needs to be something basic enough to be used without a sophisticated understanding of canine psychology. This chapter gives you such a measure. If you are an experienced trainer and/or are undertaking to train your own dog, much of this chapter will not apply to you, except that you are taking it upon yourself to meet all the conditions you would otherwise impose on a trainer.

COMPETENCE

When dog trainers talk among themselves about "methodology," they are normally referring to the mechanics of training: what kind of collar or other equipment to use, whether or not to correct a dog, or what to use for a reward—food, praise, or toy. Other questions also play a role here: in what order do you teach even the most basic commands? How much do you "show" the dog and how much do you try to get him to figure out on his own? These are all procedural matters, and frankly are less important to a service dog owner than the end result, or how competent is the dog after training. Many different methods have been proven to work on different types of dogs and in the hands of different trainers. Therefore if you are trainer-shopping, the very first thing you are interested in is the end result. In other words, be sure you understand and recognize the difference between training and testing.

Training Versus Testing

Training is a widely varied process that can involve different motivations, corrections, encouragement, help—any or all of which, in the hands of a competent trainer, are highly likely to produce a desired behavior from a dog. Sometimes this phase can look amazingly impressive even in the learning stages. But is training an accurate *test* of the dog? Not necessarily. In fact, a really good trainer can make a really bad dog look awfully cooperative. While yes, of course, you want to be impressed by a trainer's skill, you don't want the trainer to be relying on pure skill as opposed to relying on the dog. A less-skilled handler might never be able to get the dog to do the same tasks.

A Test

For a good illustration of "testing," I would strongly encourage you to attend an obedience trial, hosted by one of your local kennel clubs and associated with either the American Kennel Club or the United Kennel Club. Once there, drag your attention away from all the wonderful dogs except for the ones actually in the ring. If this is a trial (not a "fun match"), the rules in the competition ring are strict. The handler is allowed to give the dog one command for one task. The dog has a limited amount of time to respond by initiating and completing the appropriate task.

For instance, for a retrieve of the dumbbell, the handler can use any word he wants. Let's suppose he uses "fetch." The dog must wait unmoving while the handler throws the dumbbell. He cannot move until the command is given. Once the handler says "Fetch" or "Rover, Fetch" (using the dog's name with the command is acceptable), the dog must get up, move to the dumbbell, pick it up, return to the handler, and sit in front of him, again not moving until the judge instructs the handler to take the dumbbell. During this entire time, the handler is not allowed to move, speak, sway, lean, nod, gasp, laugh, or anything else that might have significance to the dog. This constitutes a *test*. One command, one response. Nothing extra. If the dog doesn't perform on this basis, he has failed the exercise and is disqualified from the class.

CHAPTER 5: UNDERSTANDING & EVALUATING TRAINING METHODS

Training In Process

Let's suppose you are interviewing a prospective trainer whom you might want to train your service dog. If he is going to show you a demonstration dog, ask him whether or not he considers this a finished dog. The answer might be "no." That's fine. Then all you can do is to see what the training process looks like for the moment—and it might be very impressive to see what he can encourage and manipulate the dog into doing. The dog's training may be complete for some commands and not for others. But at some point, you really want to see a finished product this particular trainer has produced. Is this trainer capable of showing you a dog who will give one-to-one distinct responses to single commands, without benefit of extra body language or encouragement? Keep in mind that a service dog will eventually have to maintain the working relationship with another person. He cannot rely on subtle body language cues or the trainer's degree of handling skill—what if the owner isn't as skillful?

TECHNIQUE

If you have satisfied yourself that a trainer can produce a dog who can pass a test, let's think a little more in depth about how he brought the dog to the test-passing point. Indeed, methodology is more than an issue of procedure and equipment.

Specific Limitations

While I do believe that most procedural issues are less important than the results they produce, you still have several important considerations. First, you cannot have anything happening that is harmful to the dog. That's a given and not up for debate. The second major issue is whether or not the trainer uses a technique you are capable of duplicating. If this person is going to train a dog to perform for you, then the training process, including all the applicable reinforcements, will have to be transferred to you. The dog will not enter your life with the programmed responses of a computer. You will have to develop a relationship, learn to communicate, learn to issue commands, and learn to use the correct reinforcements. If the dog has been taught only with motions or actions you cannot do, there won't be any means for you to communicate with the dog. For example, if you are a quadriplegic whose motions are limited to using your hands and wrists, controlling a dog solely by leash guidance and leash corrections probably won't be extremely practical for you.

Body Language

Many trainers develop certain body language with their canine students. They get so in the habit of using those movements that they are hardly even aware of what they are doing. For instance, a trainer might begin encouraging a dog to lie down by offering a treat on the floor. Possibly without thinking enough about it, they continue the practice of pointing to the floor when asking the dog to down. A "correction," or even a designated signal involves leaning over and pointing to the floor when the dog is to "down." While this is not necessarily terrible, if you happen to have MS or Polymysotosis, you need a method of telling the dog to down (and enforcing it if he doesn't respond) that won't land you on your head.

Personal Adaptability

These examples are, of course, very basic. Each client and each situation is completely different; the entire art of assistance dog training is grounded in the ability to adapt to individual circumstances. For real effectiveness, training absolutely must be closely evaluated and developed in relation to the individual's situation. A trainer may have had super success using prong collars, clickers, or electric collars, but it would all be completely beside the point if the client is physically unable to use any one of the three. Perhaps any one (or all) of the tools can still be used in the training process. Perhaps one or more of the devices can be modified to allow the client to use it. But at the point the dog transfers to the client, something has to transfer with him that gives the client an appropriate tool for communication and control.

COMMUNICATION GAP

Any professional trainer (or anyone evaluating the training) needs to understand the difference between obedience and submission, or conversely, disobedience and dominance—not as humans use the terms, but as they make sense to the dog.

Dogs Speak Canine

Dog "language," which contains many submissive and dominant behaviors, relates to canine psychology and is universally understood to dogs, whether or not humans understand—or agree. A dominant dog requires certain behaviors of a more submissive member of his "pack," such as: "stay out of my space," "let me sniff you anytime I want to," "I get to eat first," "I get to have whatever toys I want; you take the leftovers." Among dogs, such requirements are completely normal—and will be enforced with a physical correction from the dominant dog if necessary. In the relationships between dogs and humans, these requirements translate slightly differently, but the principle is the same. A human owner has the burden to make a dog understand, "don't bite me if I reach for your chew toy," "Don't try to grab food away from me," "Don't knock me over getting out the door first," "Don't growl at me if I tell you to get off the sofa." A huge percentage of problem pet troubles grow out of this category because humans don't understand the canine language of submission and dominance. Dogs use this language with each other throughout their lives and careers. When they cannot agree on the terms, a dog fight results. When humans get this relationship with a dog out of balance, the danger of dog bites grows as the dog attempts to do to you exactly what he'd do to another dog—apply a physical correction. What humans happen to think of the process is entirely beside the point. This is what dogs do.

Teaching the Dog to Speak Human
Obedience and disobedience relate to specific behaviors from the dog, taught by the human, that may or may not make much sense to the dog. Obedience is about getting a certain job done, and can be seen in the response a dog might give to a certain cue. (that is, Sit, Come, Fetch) These commands pertain to the human/canine relationship, but don't have much to do with a dog's natural thinking process…. Dogs don't tell other dogs to fetch a telephone. Sounds basic, yes? Well, it is, pretty much, but I find it amazingly common that folks mistake one for the other.

Does the Dog Understand the Command?
Here's an overly simplified example: let's suppose a trainer commands a dog to fetch a certain article—a keyring—by pointing to it. The dog responds by dashing off to the far side of the room to investigate a cat. The trainer goes after the dog; the dog eyes the approaching trainer and sinks to the ground with a worried look and a twitching tail. Perhaps the trainer says, "Oh, he was confused. He thought he was supposed to down." No. The dog thought he was in trouble and was handing out a strong submission signal. Did he understand the original fetch command? Was he being willfully disobedient or did he just not understand the command? Who knows? The scenario doesn't give you enough information to discern.

How Does the Dog Respond?
On the other hand, suppose when the trainer started after the dog, the dog kept running after the cat. A long and lively three-party

chase evolves. The trainer eventually recaptures the dog, and administers on-the-spot punishment (physical or verbal), which reduces the dog to the same quivering, worried down position. The trainer says, "there, that showed him. Next time he'll obey." Wrong! Find yourself a different trainer; this one is clueless. First, the dog is not offering obedience by sinking down, but submission. The original command was to fetch the keyring (which he hasn't done yet). The dog is offering submission most likely from confusion—because any "correction" applied that long after a failure to obey is completely ineffective. The dog will not connect the two. This poor dog is handing out all the signals he can think of for submission because he's getting a shellacking he doesn't understand.

How Does the Trainer Respond?

A good trainer would, indeed, go after the dog, but his response would be non-emotional and completely objective. There would be no correction because (1) the time elapsed had been too great and (2) regardless of circumstances, when a fleeing dog allows you finally to "catch" him…why would anybody correct a dog for that? It won't make him more inclined to let you catch him next time! The "catching" is what the dog will associate with the trainer's behavior because it's most recent—the last choice the dog made.

A good trainer would decide what needed to happen to produce the behavior corresponding to the initial command (fetch the keyring) and do what was necessary to ensure the behavior happened. (Incidentally, a good trainer would also recognize that he has a more foundational issue to address here than fetching keyrings; that would be a reliable "come" command!) Command/response obedience would require the trainer to back up and insist the dog follow through with the original command to fetch. However, if the dog tries to bite the trainer, or otherwise enforce his own agenda while they're working for the keyring, *now* there is dominance/submission issue! All said and done, for the purposes of assessing a reliable training program, be sure you know whether you're looking at an obedient dog or merely a submissive dog who holds a down stay because he's afraid to do anything else. (Remember the one-command/one-response test!)

ASK QUESTIONS

If you don't understand a trainer's rationale, *ask!* No good trainer will be offended. In fact, any good trainer should be thrilled, because such questions tell them they are dealing with a serious candidate who wants good, effective solutions. In fact, it is an excellent idea to ask some questions *before* observing a potential trainer working with a dog. Ask any or all of the following:

What is your objective for this session and how will you know when you achieve it? _____
_____

How do you plan to achieve the objective?_____
_____

What corrections or motivations do you plan to use? _____
_____

How long have you used that particular correction with this dog?_____
_____

What problems have you had with this dog in past sessions?
_____
_____

Remember what the trainer tells you and watch to see how well the session matches the statement of intent. If you can't understand the trainer's answer—or worse yet if he can't give you one at all—how do you expect it to make sense to the dog, who doesn't have your powers of linguistic clarification? Discrepancies might happen. Every trainer in the world has had the experience of starting a session thinking they're working on one task only to spend the whole session on something else. The dog might decide that all *his* effort is going toward avoiding the whole lesson and escaping the room. That forces a trainer to change agendas—but is also extremely obvious to an observer and should speak for itself. What you hope to see is a trainer who starts out with a clearly defined objective and has a specific plan for attaining it.

CORRECTIONS AND REWARDS

The pros and cons of training with corrections versus using strictly a system of positive reinforcement, has become a very large issue these days—large enough to merit its own chapter, so we'll discuss it more in Chapter 6. Meanwhile I would urge you to keep an open mind on the topic. Certain schools of thought would have you believe that if you allow any adversity whatsoever into the life of your dog, you are a cruel and unfeeling person. At the other end of the spectrum are those whose impatience, short tempers, or lack of understanding rely on abusive practices and dare to call it "training."

A service dog has to be a team player. For best results, he must want to work for you. This is what makes behavioral conditioning a powerful tool. But a dog is still a dog, and will always think and respond at the most basic level like....well, like a DOG! By the nature of his pack orientation, he needs to understand the psychological and physical limitations and requirements in his world. Such boundaries will make him happy and confident—not browbeaten. Such boundaries will make you much happier and confident in your service dog—and considerably safer with him in public settings.

CURRICULUM

When one starts out to build a house, there may be considerable lively debate about which tools will be necessary. What shape of hammers will we use? How heavy will they be? Will the roof be metal or shingles? Do we need more nails or screws? Certainly all of those questions need answers. But the construction crew will also need to know some information more related to overall concept. Who has the blueprints and what do they say? How long do we have? When does the inspector arrive? Consider service dog training has similar parallels. If you are fortunate enough to be dealing with a well-established training program, you should have lots of help in considering many of these issues. If you are going to choose a private trainer, you'll need to spend some time thinking about logistics.

Different trainers and programs use vastly different approaches. Quite a few programs have "boot camp" seminars to introduce clients to their dogs and cover the majority of basic instruction in a relatively short period of time—perhaps inside of two weeks. Before choosing this type of program, consider several things. Are you able to be away from home for several weeks? If necessary, is someone available to travel with you and/or to care for your home while you are away?

Becoming more common is the concept of in-home training. With this approach, dogs spend a certain amount of time being trained in a kennel and/or in the home of the trainer. Then the dog is transferred to the client's home, where training (of both client and dog) proceeds together, at regular intervals over a longer period of time. To be sure, there are advantages here, but

CHAPTER 5: UNDERSTANDING & EVALUATING TRAINING METHODS

potential disadvantages, also. Much of the training regime requires cooperation from friends and family in a way that intensive sessions away from home might not. Home scheduling can easily be as demanding as a lengthy trip away. I have participated in home-based training programs that lasted for more than a year. Talk to your potential trainer or program. Find out what will be required, and make sure you are choosing something that is possible to implement for your situation.

Less common than either previous option is having the entire training program take place while the dog lives in the client's home. While theoretically this is possible, and in certain cases perhaps even desirable, it is not the norm for most programs. If a client has training expertise, and/or if this is not his first service dog, it might be easier. If you choose this option, be aware you are signing up for an enormous project. It's rather a catch-22 that those who might most need a dog's help (and therefore be inclined to accept such an arrangement even if it was less than ideal) are often the same folks whose disability, by its practical limitations, may make them the least able to manage the demands of the program. If you live alone, cannot travel by yourself, have no help available to get in and out of your house…you may indeed desperately need the help of a dog. But before you hand over your cash, consider how you might handle the most basic of issues such as potty training and general care of the dog. Those tasks may call for the very actions in which you need a trained dog's assistance.

Finally, it's worth noting that certain types of assistance dogs are chosen as puppies and reared within the home where they are intended to work. There is a lot of risk and guesswork to such decisions, since some things about a puppy cannot be known for sure until he at least partly grown, such as whether or not he has hip or elbow dysplasia. However, there are situations that make this option attractive. As always, it becomes a study in the individual needs and circumstances.

CHECKLIST

If you are ready to interview a potential trainer, you might find the following questions helpful. Make sure you know enough to ensure results—before you choose and before you pay! Of course, you should always have a written contract in any training situation, and we'll discuss the contract specifics in Chapter 13. But before you get even close to the point of an actual contract, any trainer who claims to know enough to train a service dog should have well-thought-out answers to the following questions:

Where does the dog come from and how is he chosen? ____
_____

What are the various stages of the dog's training program and where does he stay during each of them? _____
_____

What equipment will the dog require for his job? _____
_____

Is all of this equipment something that you, or someone in your household, is capable of operating? If not, what substitutions or recommendations can the trainer make? ___
_____

How long will the training phase last in which you learn to handle the dog? Where will this take place? _____
_____

What is the procedure for obtaining follow-up help if you experience a problem in the months or years after placement? Will there be additional costs? _____

_____

SUGGESTED RESOURCES

Booth, Sheila and Gottfried Dildei. *Schutzhund Obedience: Training in Drive*. Ridgefield, CT: Podium Publications, 1992.

Cleveland, Connie. *Dogs are Problem Solvers: Complete Obedience Training, The Connie Cleveland Method*. Metamora, MI: Younglove Broadcast Services, 1999. *Note:* If you have difficulty locating these videotapes, see *www.ybsmedia.com*.

Coren, Stanley. *How to Speak Dog: Mastering the Art of Dog-Human Communication*. New York: Simon & Schuster Adult Publishing Group, 2001.

Fisher, John. *Think Dog! An Owner's Guide to Canine Psychology*. North Pomfret, VT: Trafalgar Square Publishing, 2003.

Fogle, Bruce. *Games Pets Play: How Not to Be Manipulated by Your Pet*. New York: Viking Penguin, 1987. *Note:* This book is currently out of print, but copies can usually be located on *www.abebooks.com*.

Fox, Michael W. *Superdog: Raising the Perfect Canine Companion*. New York: Simon & Schuster Adult Publishing Group, 1996. *Note:* This book is currently out of print, but copies can usually be located on *www.abebooks.com*.

Lewis, Janet R. *Smart Trainers, Brilliant Dogs*. Lutherville, MD: Canine Sports Productions, 1997.

Pryor, Karen. *Don't Shoot the Dog: The New Art of Teaching and Training*. New York: Bantam Books, 1999.

Rutherford, Clarice and David H. Neil. *How to Raise a Puppy You Can Live With*. 4th edition. Loveland, CO: Alpine Press, 2005.

Tiz, Joy. *I Love My Dog, But…: The Ultimate Guide to Managing Your Dog's Misbehavior*. New York: HarperCollins Publishers, 1999. *Note:* This book is currently out of print, but copies can usually be located on *www.abebooks.com*.

Chapter 6:
The Corrections Controversy

The C word! In today's politically correct atmosphere, few dog training topics generate as much debate as whether or not to use corrections, when, how, and what kind. Far too many people attempt to solve this debate by applying human behavioral principles to dogs. While humans and canines think much alike in many respects, it's a mistake to assume they view correction exactly as we do.

Dogs are extremely pack-oriented creatures and have been well documented as using a system of dominance and limitations with each other—and that the enforcement thereof involves physical correction. The corrections rarely escalate to a life-and-death battle when occurring within a dog's own "pack," since such fights are awfully self-defeating for the continued existence of the pack. But physical corrections themselves are common, both well-recognized and well respected, in dog-to-dog relationships. Observers can see the dominant correcting the submissive from canine infancy through adulthood in play, eating, social interactions, hunting, and even sleeping. Therefore, it is my personal position that effective interaction with dogs is going to involve one of two things: teach dogs to manage human linguistics or use their system.

CANINE CORRECTIONS

This book is not a study in canine behaviorism. The bookshelves at various stores are replete with material from qualified people about how dogs interact and "correct," thus influencing each others' behavior. I touch on the subject here only in hopes of persuading you to think about this subject, in depth, before you make any decision about a service dog. As a brief example, consider things you may have seen between two or more dogs. If you've ever observed a female with a litter, you've probably seen canine corrections. If not, have you ever seen an older dog tell a rambunctious youngster to stop climbing on him? Or to leave his chew bone alone? It's normally "verbal" at first—a growl, maybe a wrinkled lip. If the pup doesn't take the hint, the older dog is likely to grab him, abruptly and noisily, often causing the pup to shriek as though disemboweled. In most cases, though ("most" referring to interactions with a stable, well-adjusted adult dog), you'll barely find a damp hair on the puppy. The pup was told "Don't do that," a command that was very certainly explained to him by his own mother. He didn't heed, and he got the correction—which wasn't the withholding of a cookie, either.

Dogs in charge will also often tell their subordinates to take an action (not just to stop doing something). Such as MOVE out of my way. Get OUT of my bed. Go AWAY. My oldest dominant dog does this with a very specific sound that starts with a whine and ends with a growl. Of eight other dogs in my home, not a single one will fail to do exactly as she says. Immediately. With gusto. The consequences of ignoring her are a physical correction—quite forceful, even, though not harmful. In short, the pack leader decides what is and is not going to happen. There is no democratic process, no coaxing. Dogs don't use corrections among themselves for sit or down or fetch because they don't care about those behaviors. You, as the pack leader, might indeed care. Motivation is good, and very useful in training, but don't fool yourself: if you plan to be in charge, canine culture is based in corrections as well as motivations.

TRENDS IN TIMES

Not so far in the past, most dog training was a matter of imposing a system of punishments on a dog until he was bullied or coerced into doing what you wanted. Often such procedures went to the extreme and were considered very normal. Dogs—as with most animals—were considered to be expendable assets. A century ago, consideration of a the average dog's physical well being, let alone the mental, was nowhere near what is typical today.

Today, the hottest-selling training methodologies are based on operant conditioning—and sometimes incorrectly termed as such, since classic operant conditioning has four quadrants: positive reinforcement, negative reinforcement, reward, and punishment. Most modern training trends focus on positive reinforcement, with a bit of negative reinforcement thrown in. The theory is fairly basic: find what motivates the dog (food, toy, praise, etc.) and control distribution of the motivator so that it rewards the behavior you want. Voila, you are training the dog, but the dog believes he is training you. (The dog thinks: "I can make her give me a cookie just by sitting…see? Wow, doesn't she learn fast!") Everybody is happy. Behavior shaping is a powerful tool, and one that promotes one of the strongest influences of the animal kingdom: habitual behavior. Without exception, any good dog trainer knows how to use the techniques effectively. However, any service dog trainer who plans to guarantee you acceptable public performance will not limit himself *only* to positive reinforcement.

MOTIVATIONAL LIMITS

For true public reliability, a dog needs to be motivated not only by the desire to obtain a reward, but also by the knowledge that the behavior is required and that a correction will enforce if necessary. Remember our discussion in Chapter 3 about all the issues facing a "regular" dog (or even a dog intended for sports competition) being intensified in a service dog's work? A training system that relies exclusively on motivation also relies on the ability to control all circumstances in which motivation is available—and nobody can do that. You might be relying on a particular motivation when the dog decides that there is a better motivation across the street. No matter how good a trainer is, a service dog will eventually encounter "positive reinforcements" in a public setting that are far juicier than anything you provide.

PROBLEM AREAS

Take a few moments to consider some situations a service dog will face and how motivation-only training cause some problems. Since food and toys are the most commonly used rewards in motivation-only training, just think through what you're going to ask your service dog to face everyday.

Food

Let's say your service dog has been conditioned solely by the use of food, and, going one step further, even encouraged to guess at new solutions (solutions = a new behavior you want him to do) in order to obtain the food. What do you suppose might be his very logical reaction one day when you pass a restaurant buffet on which prime rib is being sliced at nose level? Or when a three-year-old wanders near with an ice-cream cone extended at arm's length? The typical random, waving arm motions of a toddler can look awfully like an invitation to any dog. What would be the plan to control a dog when he is offered food by a stranger—not only offered, but encouraged, called, and bribed?

Enticing Distractions
Okay, so forget the food, you say. Perhaps you think a dog motivated by playing with a ball would be better. Think so? If you have a dog who will sell his soul for a ball game, giving you the frozen, glazed-over expression of being willing to do anything in the world to get hold of that ball...then consider the dilemma of having a service dog somewhere that children are playing with a ball. A park with a nearby soccer game. A walk down the street of any neighborhood where a child might be in the front yard tossing a softball. You might, indeed, be able to hold onto an 70-lb dog lunging and lusting for a grip on the children's toy, but then again, maybe you can't. Do you want to chance it? Picture the large dog knocking children aside (some of whom might be terrified of the dog in the first place), grabbing the ball out of their hands, perhaps scratching arms or legs during the scuffle. Perhaps even causing a serious injury, such as a concussion or broken bone, from a fall on the sidewalk. "But he only wanted the ball," you say. "He didn't mean to hurt the child." With all due respect to you and whatever attorney you hire, I wish you luck convincing the jury. The dog is in public. He is your responsibility, period. How do you plan to ensure control of the variables?

Broad Requirements
The possibilities above are but two of thousands. Consider squirrels, fleeing cats, trips to the grocery stores, close contact with other dogs (some maybe even off leash), passers-by who might

actually seek to provoke your dog (because they think it's funny), the need for unobtrusive silence during performances or meetings, safety issues involving traffic, flying frisbees, picnics in the park... the list is literally endless. Many of the behaviors you need your dog to avoid are sufficiently self-reinforcing all by themselves to cause him to ignore the cookie you're holding. "Heck," he thinks, "I can get the cookie any time. Check out the duck in that pond!" Retrievers, for example, have been genetically selected for this focus for many generations. The odds of some of them ignoring the duck—or the nearby pigeons—in favor of a single bite of hot dog are not in your favor.

Safety

A service dog can be expected to spend nearly a decade working in public settings. The array of distractions and enticements he might face in that time is powerful, constant, and widely varied. Beyond that, 98% performance is not good enough. In some situations, there are no second chances. Consider the many parents who believe it is their small child's God-given right to approach and pet any dog in a public place. It's true that people are not supposed to do that. Yes, you can tell the parent not to allow it. But unless the parent, in a scant few seconds, is going to restrain the child and insist he stay back, guess what? You *will* have a toddler in contact with your service dog. Guess what else? If your dog raises a paw to "shake," scratching the child or even just scaring him badly, you may be in big trouble. In fact, it doesn't even have to go that far. Have you ever been thunked by the hard-wagging tail of a Labrador? Such a tail can bruise an adult's shin—let alone the unprotected eye of a toddler. Ultimately, if your dog should happen to snap at the child, or even to appear to snap, such as in grabbing something out of his hand, you could easily find yourself in court.

Such situations are one of the primary reasons Dogs For Disabled has always made huge efforts toward making a sit—with attention—an inviolable command. "Sit" means put your rear end on the ground and look at my face. Do not move for any reason until I release you. That includes other people calling you, touching you, dragging on your leash, putting pressure on your feet or tail, offering you food, tossing a ball, popping an umbrella in your face, or trying to physically push you out of a sit. All of these distractions, and dozens more, are introduced to the dog during training. From the dog's point of view, there's very little that's positively motivating about it, but cooperation is not optional.

In issues where safety is at stake—the client's, the dog's, or another person's—there is enormous value in being able to freeze the dog in place and ensure he will not move or respond. When that toddler is racing toward my dog, would I be willing to correct my dog to get a bomb-proof sit or a down? Believe it. Can a trainer guarantee the same behavior with totally positive training?

Regardless of the skill of the trainer, lack of omniscience denies us the ability to know what a dog might do if he (1) is provided the proper motivator, (2) lacks knowledge of negative consequences, (3) has not been "proofed" through a series of distractions and reinforcements. If the only reinforcements have been those of attraction to him, what happens when something else becomes more attractive? Those are long odds. Make the bet if you choose; I cannot advise it. In the United States, every person is free to make a personal choice on this matter. We are not dealing with legality, or morality. Only with practicality. But for your sake, for your dog's sake, consider carefully what you are up against.

PROBLEM TASKS

So far we've explored only the first half of the dilemma: using corrections to ensure the dog doesn't do what we want him *not* to do. Don't hurt anybody. Don't run off (especially into traffic). Don't jump on the salad bar. Don't bark during the concert. Don't urinate in the boss's office. Don't crawl under the restroom partition and offend the absolute you-know-what out of a fellow mall shopper.

What about how corrections relate to what we want to the dog to *do*? The tasks we want him to perform? It's all good and well to have a dog who loves his job. Most service dogs live the proverbial life of Reilly. Imagine how the average pet would love to spend 24 hours a day, seven days a week with his owner. Always getting to go on every ride, every trip. Utopia, yes? Well, it's a pretty good deal, but as the old saying goes, "there ain't no free lunch." Some parts of the service dog's job are less than thrilling, no matter how many treats are available. But the cold facts are that a client still needs the dog to perform, regardless of the level of enjoyment. This becomes a simple calculation in what is your first priority—the functionality and safety of the human? Or the uninterrupted enjoyment of the dog?

SEPARATING WORK FROM SPORT

When thinking through the idea of using corrections to require actions from a dog (not just to prevent undesirable actions), it is extremely important to keep certain distinctions in mind. Primarily, you need to remember that a working service dog is not competing in a sport. The majority of completely positive training techniques on the market are there to promote high scores in various types of competition—whether obedience, agility, tracking, Schutzhund, or a wide variety of other dog-related sports.

Agility and Confidence

Watching a well-trained dog zoom about an agility course is a beautiful and thrilling sight. They leap hurdles, balance on high walkovers, scale A-frame walls, and dive through tight tunnels. In a sporting contest, this is about speed, accuracy, attention, and athleticism. In a real-life job this might be about balancing correctly and navigating a rubble pile in the wake of an earthquake or a bomb blast. Athleticism, focus, and attention—with all possible speed. Someone's life depends on it.

Searching and Rescuing

Scent tracking tests are fascinating events. Dogs compete on various levels from very basic (about 300 paces with several articles to find along the way) to extremely long, complex tracks with loop-backs, crossovers by other people, and multiple objects they must notice and indicate. Dogs are scored on exact precision, how close they stay to the track, how reliably they indicate the article. Depending on the level being tested, the handler may or may not know where the track is. In a real life job, the handler won't have a clue. He must follow his dog up hill and down dale, over any number of obstacles or terrain, reading his body language correctly and having confidence in the dog's ability to find that lost hiker or missing child before it's too late. Someone's life depends on it.

Performance and Life Tasks

Unless you've tried it, describing the demands of attaining a top-level competitive obedience performance is almost impossible. The process requires energy, attitude, and the ability to hone every skill to achieve tiny fractions of points. To get a dog to maintain a precise position consistently, to move with animation, and show enthusiasm for every command—this is an art form in itself. It requires enormous skill, tremendous discipline, and great patience.

But for the purposes of a service dog, we're dealing in apples and oranges. A "fetch" exercise in a competition places as much merit on *how* the dog gets the dumbbell as on whether or not he actually comes back to you with it. How fast does he move? How quickly does he grab it? Does he hold it properly? Does he sit straight in front of you when he returns or is he off to the side? A fast, precise competitive retrieve is a beautiful thing to watch and is a lovely demonstration both of training skill and of the dog's character. It does not, however, have a single thing to do with whether or not a dog will fetch the cordless telephone when someone has fallen upside down in the bathtub and can't get out. A life may depend on that.

What is the point here? When searching for a service dog trainee, remember that *you* may be one of those whose life depends on the dog's performance. Exactly that upside-down-in-the-bathtub scenario is why Dogs For Disabled has a motto for their phone-fetch training: "The first time, every time." Meaning that a finished dog has to respond correctly every single time, regardless of circumstances or level of distraction. Safety, perhaps even a life, is at stake. Whether the dog sits straight when he brings you the phone, or whether he holds it by the middle or the end, is pretty immaterial. Getting that result may require using corrections during training.

TEACHING CORRECTIONS

Moving on, if you want to hire a trainer who knows how to use corrections effectively, how do you choose? More to the point, exactly what are you choosing? First let's dispense with notions of abuse. By referring to corrections, I mean nothing, absolutely nothing, that would cause physical harm to a dog.

To best define a correction, I need to borrow some quotes and some methodology from Connie Cleveland, the founder of the Dogs For Disabled program. Connie has told thousands of people that "corrections are not random acts of violence." To merit distinction from abuse, a correction must meet certain conditions.

A dog must demonstrate by his behavior that he clearly understands a correction, by his ability to do two things:

- avoid the correction entirely, and
- "turn the correction off" after it has started.

Deliberate Control

If you encounter a trainer whose idea of correction is to slap the dog around and/or yank him off his feet for every failure to perform, don't walk away—run. This sort of behavior is not "technique" at all, but is utter abusive nonsense and exactly what gives a horrid reputation to any concept of corrections in training. No appropriate correction happens because of a trainer's frustration or anger. Not ever.

A proper correction is a controlled, specific action, and is always applied with objectivity and deliberation. The corrective action is gradually and carefully introduced to the dog over a period of time in a way that predisposes him to the correct response and repeatedly shows him how to "win," meaning to make the action stop. The correction is never any stronger than the lowest level possible to obtain the dog's attention and cooperation.

The Learning Process

Personally, I have little patience with *teaching* with corrections. I believe that teaching (introducing or inducing desired actions) is definitely a place for behavioral conditioning—to encourage the dog to guess at behaviors until he figures out the "right" answer. To do otherwise is to cause a dog to fear to try. Call it bribery,

CHAPTER 6: THE CORRECTIONS CONTROVERSY

call it "showing," call it predisposing behavior. I don't care what you want to call it. A good trainer can teach a dog to associate a word with an action using the dog's own actions and desires. Corrections should be introduced as a reinforcement only *after* the dog has demonstrated his ability to connect the cue (spoken word or other action) with the related behavior. (Yes, we're getting a bit technical here, and this is not a training manual, per se. However, clients or sponsors should understand enough theory to make good choices.)

The Transition

As an example, almost any dog with a reasonable amount of "play drive," (what many dog trainers call "prey drive") can be taught to "fetch" a tennis ball because it's fun. "Fetch" becomes a known sound for a certain action, and the dog is normally glad to do it. But it's a long step from a dog's recognition of "fetch" the tennis ball that's bouncing across the yard to having a dog who can be relied on to "fetch" your car keys out of a scummy, slimy puddle that's half underneath your vehicle. In the rain. In the dark. In a nasty, scary part of town. At that point, I'm willing to bet you won't have a lot of concern about how much fun you think the dog is having. He's not, and neither are you. But if you're the one in the wheelchair with only a dog for company, you'll be needing those car keys without any delays or debate about how many cookies are involved. Getting that degree of reliability in a dog's response will almost certainly require a corrective training process.

The Specific Action

When we refer to corrections, what specific actions are we discussing? The answer must depend on the dog and on the abilities of the client. As examples, the most common corrections used in the Dogs for Disabled training regime are pressure on the leash, tugs ("pops") on the leash, an ear pinch (flat fingered), and an appropriate level of stimulus from an electric collar. In most cases, all the needed behaviors to perform any number of service dog tasks can be taught with this set of corrections. Often with two or three of the four. Depending on the abilities of the client, the corrective action may have to be altered. For instance, if a prospective client has no ability to grip a leash, training a dog with a leash correction is pretty pointless. That client needs something else he can use effectively.

In all cases, every "correction" is introduced to the dog in such a way that it is gentle, low-key, and part of a very deliberate process. In the beginning, it is barely strong enough to notice. How strong the correction ultimately needs to get to guarantee performance depends on the nature of the dog. Each dog is carefully predisposed to give the proper response. Praise is lavish. Sessions are short. I have always found it very interesting to see that some politically savvy trainers refer to this very process as "teaching a motivation," when in fact they are every bit as much teaching a dog to avoid a stimulus as to do an action. The "motivation" consists of evading the correction. Terminology is not important! Make pragmatism your standard, not semantics: *does it work??*

Advance Planning

Since this book is not a training manual, it's impossible to explore this topic fully. For our purposes here, I merely want to assure the dubious that a correction is not something you try when everything else has failed or because you don't know what else to do. *Teaching corrections is a deliberate process that happens long before you ever need to rely on them.*

Over the years, at times I've mentioned to many people that Dogs For Disabled teaches a compulsive retrieve using (usually) an ear pinch as a correction, I've often heard versions of the following response. "Oh, that's a bad idea. It didn't work for my dog. I was having trouble with a retrieve, so one day I pinched my dog's ear. He didn't retrieve—he tried to bite me." At such moments I have to stifle the urge to respond, "Good. How sensible of your dog." That's not training. That's random behavior, and it is totally incomprehensible to your dog for any training purpose.

If you are shopping for a trainer, and have decided on one who uses corrections, part of your interview should be a request for them to explain, and demonstrate, to you how they *introduce* corrections. The trainer should not only have a ready answer that makes sense, but he should be able to show you a dog who responds to specific, defined "corrections" with specific actions—without getting agitated, stressed, or otherwise hysterical.

ELECTRIC COLLARS

Both for fear of being misunderstood and for fear of clients overlooking an extremely valuable tool, it's necessary to follow up on my earlier comment about electric collars. It's easy to find places and trainers who believe electric collars are tools of the very devil. Beyond that, it's not very hard to find trainers who use electric collars in horribly inappropriate ways and richly deserve the bad reputation. But if you are truly needing the most reliable work from a dog, and want the most fair, most deliberate, least emotional method of guaranteeing performance, I would urge you to do some research. Electric collars are, like any other piece of equipment, a tool. They can be used appropriately or inappropriately. Effectively or not. Humanely or not. The issues of correct use and training methods are impossible to address fully here, but here are some thoughts to consider.

Equivalent Correction

However, I will go on record as saying that all dogs graduating from Dogs For Disabled go through "collar conditioning," or learning to understand corrections from an electric collar as part of training. This is not a matter of attempting to punish a dog away from a poor behavior. The collar is carefully worked into training as an attention correction in the same way a handler might use a tug on a leash. The name itself, "electric" collar, is not even completely accurate, since several types *operate* via electricity…but the "correction" delivered to the dog is not a shock at all—only a vibration or a tone.

The governing principle is not the ability to deliver a correction more severe than that from a leash, but the ability to deliver a correction from a greater distance than possible with a leash and with minimum body motion from the trainer. Strength of correction from any tool is a matter of trainer choice; in fact, electric collars can provide a perfectly-consistent correction that's actually far *milder* than ones from some training collars. The value of the tool is so high as to be incalculable, especially when considering that many clients are physically unable to use other corrections.

Remote Control

The ability to apply corrections from a distance has a value that is hard to overstate. An electric collar essentially provides "remote control." A correction that could normally be made only when a dog is on leash is now available from one end of the house or yard to another. Whether or not the client handling the dog ever lays a finger on the electric collar, a competent trainer with a cheap radio ear piece and the remote control can provide more backup to a struggling client in five minutes than days' worth of treat tossing or leash tugging. One of my favorite places for putting this method into practice has been a two-level shopping mall where I could follow along the upper balcony, and the dog would not know I was nearby. Careful instruction to the client and close observation by the trainer can make the dog believe firmly in the client's omnipotent ability to correct him.

Other Advantages

Ultimately, an electric collar can provide a far more effective correction than any other tool. You can vary the intensity of the correction to almost any level—far less, in fact, than the force of a leash correction. The correction is consistent: it's always the same. It's specific: it does not depend on body movement or being in a correct position. Timing is much more precise: it does not rely on the varying coordination of the handler.

DECISIONS

I can only hope that no one finishes this chapter with the impression I am advocating a zero-quality life for the dog, solely for the benefit of a human. As already stated, I am entirely opposed to any type of correction that would bring harm to a dog. And I am entirely in favor of an enjoyable, mutually-fulfilling relationship between human and dog. I also believe that result happens only when the dog clearly understands his boundaries and tasks, and is confident in the established pack order: human at top, dog below.

I also have stressed repeatedly that this book is not an attempt to convert the world to my point of view. Please understand this is particularly important when it comes to corrections. You have to choose what works for you, and you are the one who must be comfortable—and functional—with the choice. My goal is for you to make informed choices that work for *you*.

Whether you are a service dog user, a breeder, a trainer, a sponsor, or merely an interested bystander, I urge you to think through the situation before making a decision or pronouncing any sweeping judgements. Not only are the people all different, the dogs are all different too. There is no principle of correction or training that doesn't, at least occasionally, need modification to suit a specific situation. Ultimately, the responsibility is your own. Research. Observe. Ask for examples and demonstrations. Evaluate critically. Ask questions. No trainer with confidence in himself and his methods will be offended by questions.

Decide what you are willing to do as well as what you are able to do (physically, practically, emotionally). Choose a trainer who uses a compatible method. If you are unwilling to use a physical correction, spend your time and money on a dog who has been taught exclusively with positive reinforcement. If you plan to use corrections, don't buy a dog from someone who has used only positive reinforcement and then start applying corrections that the dog has never been taught to understand. Neither route is fair to anyone. I've seen plenty of people make one error or the other, then blame the trainer because the dog "doesn't work."

Corrections constitute an issue you need to decide ahead of time, not on the basis of emotion or aesthetic preference and not in the middle of a crisis. The decision should be based on practical merit. Determine what the dog needs to do, how you plan to make sure the tasks happen, and what measures you are willing to take to ensure success—while at the same time, ensuring the safety of those around you and of the dog himself.

SUGGESTED READING

Cleveland, Connie. *Understanding Corrections*. 1998-2005. 23 May 2005. <www.dogtrainersworkshop.com/dtw14.asp>

_____. *Escape Behavior.* 1998-2005. 23 May 2005. <www.dogtrainersworkshop.com/dtw18.asp>

Rutherford, Clarice and David H. Neil. *How to Raise a Puppy You Can Live With*. 4th edition. Loveland, CO: Alpine Press, 2005.

Chapter 7:

The Job Description

What exactly can a service dog do? Clients may find much confusion afoot about what a dog can (or cannot) be trained to do. This is a complex topic, but certainly the most important. All other considerations are secondary. Most of the other analyses or decisions are means to an end—questions of logistics, preferences, and practicality. This topic is the "end." The actual objective. You would have no reason to explore financing, travel options, training types, etc., if there is no hope of actually getting the dog to do the job you need done.

As with all questions about service dogs, the verdict on what a dog can or can't do will get different answers from different trainers. Some of the differences may come from varying levels of experience or skill. Some differences may have to do with service dogs' amazing ability to expand and adapt their training after placement. However, what we want to establish here is the concrete. What can a dog be trained and required to do on the basis of specific commands alone? As a common example, suppose you want your service dog to fetch a certain item in your house on command. We've used that "phone" command for lots of examples, so let's use it again.

Can the dog be taught to fetch the telephone any time you tell him to do so? Yes, he can. Additionally, it might be interesting to consider that after a certain amount of time the dog might learn to associate the ring as a precursor to the command, and start fetching the phone any time it rings. However, that's extra (unless you plan to use the ring itself as a command and teach it that way). The original task was to bring the cordless in response to the command "phone." That action is a specific task. Our goal in this chapter is identify which tasks your dog can definitely be taught to do and provide some clarification about tasks in the "maybe" category.

First let's narrow our focus a bit. We've already discussed some different types of training, but for the purpose of this chapter's discussion, we are going to ignore technique. Regardless of whether a trainer uses corrections, treats, prong collars, or head collars in this chapter we're referring only to the end product: a dog that recognizes certain cues to perform corresponding behaviors. We are not debating training methodology, but trying to outline and analyze the job itself.

BREEDS AND JOBS

At the very outset, let's have a word about breeds. All dogs are dogs, of course, but breed characteristics are enormously important. Choice of breed can play a huge role in the success or failure of any dog for a given job. At the most basic level, if you want a dog to pull a wheelchair, he has to be large enough. If you want a dog to provide balance during walking, he needs to be the correct height. If you plan for your dog to retrieve lots of papers and other delicate objects, don't choose a dog with the well-known "shoestring drool"! Considerations are widely varied; you will serve yourself best by giving much thought to which breed(s) have the best predisposition to the behavior you desire. Chapter 9 discusses breed selection more thoroughly. Here we have to assume we're at least beyond the obvious, such as whether or not a Papillon can pull your wheelchair or whether or not a 50-pound dog can pick up a 200-pound man from the floor.

REALISM

Stories abound of dogs who perform astounding feats for their owners. Some readers may remember the TV feature in the mid-1990s of the Irish Setter dialing 911 to help its owner. In the wake of that program—and the tidal wave of pleas for similar dogs—a lot of trainers were pounding their heads on walls for about a year. Is this kind of thing valid or not? How can you know?

Okay, you've had a fabulous idea. You, or someone in your family, is disabled. What if a dog could be trained to assist with the one task that makes your daily routine so frustrating? Your hopes are soaring, but five phones calls to different trainers in the yellow pages have given you five different answers. "No problem!" Says one trainer…but the price is staggering. And why does he sound like something hard will be so easy? (And, by the way, if it is so darned easy, then why is it so darned expensive?)

"Impossible," says the next trainer…but she sounds like she doesn't really want to be bothered.

Whoa. Stop everything. Forget the random opinion approach. Forget all the trainers and their advertisements. Let's realign our thinking a bit. You need a concrete starting point, followed by a breakdown of the actions involved in the task, to figure out if each one is teachable—and enforceable—to the dog.

TASKS

Use the lines below to write a few sample tasks you want a service dog to perform. We're going to be specific and concrete, remember? Here are a couple of examples:

Example Task #1:
> While I am sitting in my wheelchair, the dog should go to the other side of the room, pick up the TV remote control and bring it to me.

Example Task #2:
> While I am lying in bed, the dog should go through the nearby doorway into the bathroom and turn on the light.

Write your sample tasks below:

_____
_____
_____
_____
_____

Now, answer these yes/no questions about each task you wrote above, even if they seem repetitive (they're not) or so basic as to be a waste of your time (you might be surprised):

- Y/N Would the task allow a verbal or physical command to be given to the dog?

- Y/N Is the person who needs to initiate the task physically capable of giving a command or cue?

- Y/N Is the action needed within the realm of physical possibility for a dog? (that is, does not require thumbs, literacy, or 300 pounds of muscle)

Y/N   Can the situation in which the task is needed be recreated at will for training purposes? (note that seizures cannot)

Y/N   Is the action the dog needs to take observable to the handler?

Y/N   Is the dog always within the handler's sight while he is performing the task?

If every answer is "yes," you can be pretty sure a dog can be trained for the job. If you have a "no" cropping up here and there, we'll need to take a closer look. That's not to say the task is impossible, or that the dog cannot help. But the process needs careful evaluation.

INDIVIDUAL ACTIONS

All right, put your list aside for a moment. We'll come back to it in a little while. For the moment, let's practice thinking like a dog.

Canine Perception

We have to consider what the commands we teach actually mean to a dog. Dogs don't speak or think in English or any other verbiage of homo sapiens. In addition, they are much more situation-specific than people. Therefore, when they respond to a command, how do they perceive the action they are taking? For example, when you tell a dog to "heel," does he see that as an action he is going to do? Or as a location where he is going to go? *What?* you say….Why does it matter?! While this might seem like splitting the proverbial hair, it's a pretty important hair, especially to your dog.

Don't believe it? If you, like many people, have taught your dog to "heel" on walks (in other words, not to drag you when on leash), try this. Attach a leash to his collar while he is standing in front of you. Stand still. Now tell him to "heel," but don't move. What does he do? Anything? Lacking more specific training, chances are pretty good he'll just stand there and stare back at you. He's probably waiting for you to do your part (Move!) so he can "heel." Can he adjust this knowledge to learn that "heel" is a place (by your side, facing forward) that he has to get in and stay in whether you are standing still, walking, or sitting? Absolutely. Ask anyone who does competitive obedience. But at the moment, to him, the action he associates with that word is one of motion. Not of going to a location.

Terminology

Now, here's the important part: it does not matter what word means which action. *What matters is that YOU understand what each individual word means to the dog.* The significance is not in the term itself. To you, they are vocabulary terms with definitions. To your dog, they are just different sounds. The significance of the split hair is understanding exactly what *physical action* a specific command signifies to the dog.

When the telephone rings and you say "phone," your dog has no concept of you communicating with another person by holding that thing to your head and talking. What does he see himself doing by bringing the phone to you? Well, that's just retrieving to him, albeit perhaps retrieving of a particular object. But overall, it's just one more idiosyncrasy of these odd humans—one more occasion to pick up this hard plastic thing and take it to The Boss. The basic concept is little different to him than picking up the pen you dropped underneath the desk.

CHAPTER 7: THE JOB DESCRIPTION

COMBINATIONS OF ACTIONS

A dog's view of tasks may be more simplified than ours, but his view is still an effective means of communication. Individual commands are what make it possible for a service dog owner to apply a basic training to a wide variety of situations. At Dogs for Disabled, we call this "Building Block Training." As such, it creates flexibility and makes it possible for a dog to perform complex tasks that he could not otherwise possibly comprehend.

One Word = One Action

In early stages of training, physical actions have a one-to-one correlation with a single word, just as we noted above regarding the "heel" command. "Sit." "Down." "Come." One command nets one action. In more complex assignments, a service dog near the end of his training can perform functions that are a combination of many single commands.

Furthermore, as that chain of individual commands is repeated, a dog learns to anticipate a complex task according to the circumstances and act accordingly. A good example is that of a dog learning to open a weighted door for someone in a wheelchair. A finished dog is capable of moving to the correct position by the chair, pulling the door open by a special apparatus containing a braided strap, holding the door while the person enters, switching from the braided strap to the nylon cord, releasing the device, returning the device to the owner, and resuming a correct position by the chair. A dog performing this function is responding to a sequence of 10 separate commands (some repeated at different places in the sequence). After a while, it all blends into a single process, but it is *taught* one task at a time, the individual commands being:

    1 *Heel:* go to the left side of the chair.

    2 *Stand:* stand up.

3 *Pull:* take the braided leather strap in your mouth and apply pressure.
4 *Get back:* back up.
5 *Hold:* stay still, maintain pressure on the strap (dog may sit if it is easier for him).
6 *Okay:* release the pressure.
7 *Drop:* let go of the strap.
8 *Take it:* take the nylon cord in your mouth, pull the device off the door handle, and bring it to me.
9 *Heel* or *side:* return to the desired position by the chair.
10 *Drop:* let go of the cord.

A fully-trained, seasoned dog will recognize the sequence the moment he sees the doorstrap appear and normally requires only three prompts: "Pull" (telling him when to start), "hold" (telling him how far to open the door), and "okay" (telling him when he can finish the sequence). If, several years in the future, a dog decides door opening is no longer in his contract, a trainer can always return to the individual commands to fix the problem.

Adaptable Actions

Even though the dog anticipates one particular process, he still knows each individual command as a specific action. Therefore the commands have significance far beyond any one task. In a correctly-trained dog, specific commands are generalized to apply to varied situations. With canine graduates of Dogs for Disabled, for example, "Take it" means pick up anything I point to (either with my finger or with a laser pointer) and bring it to me. "Pull" means grab hold of whatever I'm pointing to and pull on it until I tell you to stop. With a dog that has been taught to pull (often on a tab of leather or cord, but not always) an owner can expand this to mean anything he wants it to mean. *Pull* the hamper from the bedroom to the laundry area. *Pull* the drawer open. *Pull* the bathroom door shut. *Pull* the shower curtain closed. *Pull* the wheelchair over here to the side of my bed. *Pull* my sock off. *Pull* the blanket out of the dryer. *Pull* the garbage cart to the curb. These are very different jobs to a human, but they're all the same concept to the dog. If you're doing laundry, the dog has nary a notion about whether or not you have clean socks for tomorrow or what wash cycle to use. He's just pulling.

Name-Specific Actions

The extension to this principle is something name-specific, such as a telephone or a purse you want the dog to bring to you when you ask for it by name. The actual name of the object would be taught in conjunction with the retrieve command (that is, "Fetch the phone"). Eventually "Fetch" would be phased out and "Phone" becomes a reference to retrieving a particular object. But guess what...so far as the dog is concerned, he is STILL *fetching!*

Action Vocabulary

Below is an average "vocabulary list" taught to dogs graduated from the Dogs for Disabled program; this list would be typical for dogs being placed with a handler who uses a wheelchair. For each command, a general description of the corresponding action is given. Depending on the specifics of their situation and routine, most owners can expand the impact of each command far beyond that of basic training.

Let's Go	Walk next to me, or keep up with me.
Sit	Put your rear end on the ground and look at me.

No	Whatever you're doing, QUIT. This command is reserved for correcting behavior that is always wrong, not just incorrect for the moment. "Don't do it again in this lifetime."
Leave it	Leave that alone. Don't touch it.
Stand	Move to the standing position and stay still (even if I put pressure on you by pulling or bracing).
OK	Release command—especially for stays or holds.
Come	Come to the handler ("Come" is also a position. See below.)
Heel	Sit on the left of the chair or handler. The dog should be parallel to the handler facing straight ahead.
Side	Sit on the right side of the chair or handler. The dog should be parallel to the handler facing straight ahead.
Front	Come to the right front of the chair. The dog should be positioned between the right armrest and the handler's right knee and should face the handler.
Come	Come to the left front of the chair. The dog should be positioned between the left armrest and the handler's left knee and should face the handler.
Take it	Pick that up and bring it to me.

Drop	Let go of whatever is in your mouth.
Look	Look away from me and find the laser pointer dot. There's something out there I want you to do.
Yes!	Used to indicate to the dog that he is picking up correct item.
Uh-Uh	Do not pick that up or that's not what I want you to do right now. This is **not** a correction. Just "nice try, wrong answer." A no-reward marker.
Go	Move away from me toward the area I'm pointing to.
Move	Get yourself somewhere else. Get out of the way of my feet, walker, or chair.
Get In	Get in house, crate, car, etc.
Wait	"Not yet" or "freeze." Stop moving and wait for another command.
Down	Lie down.
Stay	Remain where you are until I come back to you.
Place	Go to and stay on your bed. You don't have to lie down, but stay on the bed.
Up	Stand up on the counter, table, wall, door, etc.
Hug	Stand up with your front feet on my lap. Stand still.

Off	Put four feet on the floor. Off my lap, off the edge of a counter, off the bed.
Pull	Take the indicated object in your mouth and pull on it.
Forward	Pull the wheelchair, from either right or left side.
Easy	Slow down.
Get Back	Back up (Allow handler through a door or narrow opening first, or back up while you're pulling on the doorstrap).
Stop	Cease moving forward, plus resist forward motion of the chair.
Quiet	Stop barking (whining, screaming, yodeling…).
Hurry up	Go to the bathroom (on leash).
Lights	Turn the lights on or off with your mouth.
Touch	Apply pressure to an object with your paw (light switch, door opener, elevator button).
Phone	Go get the cordless telephone from its special place and bring it to me.
Speak	Bark until I tell you Quiet. Helpful as an alert to a family member or neighbor or as a signal for help in public.
Push	Nudge this with your nose (close a drawer, put my foot back on a footrest).

Vocabulary Sequencing

As a starting point for in-home training, this list gives the handler control of 38 different physical actions from his dog. Each action is individual, observable, and reinforceable and can, therefore, be combined to work in different sequences to accomplish different tasks, such as previously described in the opening of a weighted door. Here is another example that could be "built" from the basic command list: "Answering the door." The door bell rings. (*Look, go, touch* or *pull*) The dog activates a camera or speaker so the handler can verify the caller's identity. (*Sit*) The dog sits and stays still while the handler talks to the visitor. (*Pull* or *touch*) the dog opens the door by pulling on a strap or activating a switch (*Come* or *Place*) dog moves away from the open door and away from the visitor to the desired location.

How far can this approach be applied? Over time, with consistent handling, amazingly far. I've seen service dogs walk out with only basic task-training and after a few months of handling by a determined owner, the dog is fetching drinks from the refrigerator, loading the washing machine, and dragging recycling bins to the curb. I believe my personal favorite was the dog who learned to start his owner's customized van on winter mornings. The owner unlocked the van with a remote entry device and observed the rest from the comfort of the warm house. Fortunately for her goal, the ignition happened to be a push-button type and the entry doors had lever handles to which tabs could be attached. (This was considerably before the days of remote ignition being common.) Her dog's sequence of tasks included *go, look, pull, drop, get in, touch, come, wait, look, pull, drop, come.* Think that one through! It was a pretty sophisticated accomplishment for a 22-year-old woman with her first dog ever. In the end, all she had to do was open the front door and say "go." The dog would dash to the van, open the door, start the vehicle, close the door, and return to the house.

Training Thought

Time out, please! Although this is not a training book, per se, if you are a trainer reading this book to gain perspective and ideas, I can't resist the urge to add a brief, parenthetical bit just for you: teach your task sequences backwards. In the human mind, it may make more sense to start at the beginning, but it does not to the dog. I have heard Dogs for Disabled founder, Connie Cleveland, tell scores of students, "Move from what the dog does *not* know, into what he *knows*. Make the goal apparent to him." Dogs anticipate (especially willing, eager to please dogs—a typical service dog), so set him up to anticipate the correct end result. Connie's method of teaching a retrieve is a classic example, beginning with teaching the delivery: this object is in your mouth—give it to me. Then we back up into holding the object first. Then in picking it up and holding it. Then in holding it at a greater distance, returning to me, and delivering it. Then moving out to the greater distance, picking it up, followed by return and delivery.[1] The dog builds confidence as he discovers the job gets easier, not harder. Start with the objective; back up and add in the additional steps one at a time, in reverse order.

Task Backfire

A word of warning: creativity is often required! Imagine the Catch-22 created by teaching a dog how to open the refrigerator or a step-operated trash can. I wrestled this dilemma with my very first trainee during my apprenticeship. The retriever in question had no trouble extrapolating his technique for the purposes of self-serving

---

[1] For further information on this method of teaching a compulsive retrieve, go to Connie Cleveland's web site at *www.dogtrainersworkshop.com*.

on refrigerated leftovers. He did me out of quite a few groceries until I came up with a solution. What eventually worked for him were two identical door-opening devices. One that was kept on top of the refrigerator for the times that I actually asked him to open the door. The other was kept on the fridge door, well-soaked in bitter apple. It took a while (and some sneakiness on my part) to make a believer out of him, but eventually we did strike a helpful balance: the cord is nasty until I tell you to open it; then the bad taste magically disappears.

NON-REINFORCEABLE TASKS

Alas, there is a qualifier (isn't there always?). Building Block Training is grounded in specific, individual behaviors. Each sequence is made up of individual actions that can be praised or reinforced one action at a time. But remember our list of yes/no questions? So far, we have dealt only with those tasks to which all of the answers are "yes." All of the individual pieces are observable to the handler, can be set up with all variables any time you want to practice, and allow specific commands. A huge change of footing looms when one wants a dog to perform tasks that are not observable to a handler and/or have to happen without a direct command.

"Commands" from the Environment

It is possible to teach a dog that something from his surroundings constitutes a command. This is the process through which a hearing assistance dog alerts to sounds. The operative question is whether or not the handler is also able to perceive the environmental "command" and subsequently know whether or not the dog is performing correctly. In other words, if a person cannot hear, and the dog decides to take the afternoon off instead of responding to a doorbell…short of a visual cue, how can the handler require the behavior or correct the lack of response?

From the practical perspective, this is the same dilemma faced by pet owners whose dog kitchen-counter shops when they're out of the house. You, personally, cannot reinforce (positively or negatively) behaviors that happen outside your presence or awareness. How a dog performs in such circumstances, and/or what he is capable of being taught to do, relies on factors outside your direct control. Trainers must improvise, use circumstances within the environment to cue or control the dog—and hope they've correctly chosen a dog with lots of initiative.

Seizure Responses

One of the most common areas in which this question arises has to do with seizures or brain injuries. While it is definite fact that some dogs alert their owners to impending seizures, it is (so far) a myth that dogs can be *trained* to alert to seizures. They can, indeed, be *trained to respond* to seizures. And it is also true that training a dog to respond to a seizure can predispose him to perform an alert—especially after a good bond is established with the handler.
But it is important not to confuse the two events. Despite all the accomplishments of modern science, it is not yet possible to know exactly what a dog is "alerting" *to*. Is it scent? Electro-magnetic? Subtle body language? In many cases we cannot even know from a medical point of view, what is causing a person's seizure. Nor, even if we did, can we (or would we!) recreate the seizure at will for the purpose of training.

What *can* be done is to train the dog to make a specific response to a specific behavior. For example, if a seizure for a particular person results in a convulsion, a trainer is going to have to successfully imitate the convulsion and teach the dog an appropriate response. *Bark* to alert a family member? *Pull* to activate an alarm to someone outside the house? (Of course, the action has to be chosen based on the individual situation. It's no good for the dog merely to bark for help if the owner lives alone.) Once a response is established, it's possible that the correct dog with good training and a good bond, will begin to anticipate the seizure by initiating the trained response before the owner is aware, and/or while the owner is still conscious.

Response Adaptation

How do the dogs know? So far humans have lots of theories, but no demonstrable facts. Beware if someone guarantees you they can train a dog to alert to your seizures. Even if this trainer can show you a dog who clearly alerts to a seizure (proving it by videotape or some such means), there remains a logical problem. Who can say whether or not your seizures would be identical to those the dog is currently anticipating? Again, until we can verify to what symptoms a dog is reacting, the response anticipation cannot be guaranteed. However, a dog trained in a particular *response* to an actual seizure is of great value for that function alone. Plus there is a very real chance that he will, in time, teach himself how to do an advance alert.

My first personal experience with this phenomenon involved a woman, Lucy, who had been critically injured in a car accident, resulting in brain injury and subsequent blackouts. Sometimes she could feel them coming on because of some dizziness and disorientation. Sometimes there was no advance warning. The dog, Emma, an Australian Shepherd, was taught a verbal command to get help at times when Lucy had warning. Emma's method of getting help was via a "bringsel," a special object (in this case a large bandana with a certain spice tied inside) which she was to take to another member of the family. That was a signal Lucy was not feeling well and anticipating problems. (Just

CHAPTER 7: THE JOB DESCRIPTION

for clarification, the spice meant nothing to the family member, but it helped Emma distinguish the bandana from another incidental handkerchief or sock.)

Emma's task was practiced a good deal in the initial weeks of her placement, not always in connection with any difficulties, but just to ensure that it was functional and understood by all parties. Sometimes, of course, it was necessary for the real reason. Lucy and her family experienced the normal amount of complications and small troubles while everyone learned to work together. Eventually everything smoothed out and the performance was reliable. With a frequency of perhaps twice a week, Lucy would send Emma to fetch her husband when she sensed any dizziness. They also experienced a few situations where Lucy blacked out without warning.

One day about four months following Emma's placement, Lucy was sitting at her desk balancing a checkbook when Emma jumped up from her nearby bed, snatched the handkerchief from Lucy's pocket, and disappeared. Since Lucy had a tendency to mutter to herself while working, she wondered if she'd said something that Emma interpreted as a command. She stood up to follow the dog, and met her husband coming inside. Right in the middle of saying, "I don't know why she did that; everything is fine," Lucy blacked out and fell into her husband's arms. A new era had begun. Emma was now—as proved by her subsequent actions—an alert dog. If I could tell you how she anticipated the problem, I'd be a very wealthy individual! But the truth is much less satisfying: we simply do not know. What we do know is to teach the dog the best *response* possible and hope that the dogs' wonderful, innate senses take care of the rest.

Service dogs and their owners experience similar scenarios quite often. Often they're not quite as dramatic, but the concept is little different. The dog discussed at the beginning of this chapter—

the one who dialed 911 for its owner—had most likely been trained to knock the phone off the hook and to "touch" the keypad. Perhaps every button on that phone was speed-dial programmed for 911. I do not know; I was never able to find out. I will promise you that the dog did not calculate the handler's vital signs, assess the need for medical support, and read/push the numerals 9-1-1 on the keypad. In one way or another, the dog was making a previously-conditioned response, just as Emma did with Lucy's bandana.

Commands versus Adaptation

So, to draw a few more parallels for clarification: a dog can be taught to activate (by button or pull-cord) a security alarm for moments when you think someone is breaking into your house. But he won't decide to do it because he hears someone in the back yard. For all he knows, it could be the meter reader or the garbage collector. You'll have to give him a cue to activate the alarm.

A dog can be taught to bark an alert if your autistic child opens the front door, so long as you can recreate the situation enough times, in your presence, to appropriately teach and reinforce. But if you want the dog to provide this alert in the middle of the night while you are sleeping—you will have to rely on innate responsibility taking over the trained response. Probable? Yes. Guaranteed? No.

A dog can be taught a command to fetch another member of the household if you feel ill or hurt yourself in someway. But if you fall and hit your head and lose consciousness, there is no guarantee that the dog is going to dash off to find help. Might he know that you're in trouble and take the initiative? Yes, he might. You cannot know, and neither can I. On the other hand, he might also think you're taking a nap and curl up contentedly beside you. This situation would go on the list of ones that are pretty difficult to recreate for the purposes of training. Again, possible? Yes. Guaranteed? Not necessarily.

NON-OBSERVABLE ACTIONS
Similar in concept, but a little different in application, are the matters of tasks a dog needs to do which take him out of your sight. One factor different from many non-enforceable actions is that you can often recreate this situation at will for training. That helps. But you might need to get creative—or even a little sneaky.

Out of Sight is Out of Reach
Consider what might happen with this question: "Can my dog be taught to go to the front door to let my nurse or aide inside before I get up? Because I cannot get out of bed without help." Answer: "Sure. Teachable—yes. Enforceable—a little more tricky. What if one night you forgot to put up your snacks, and the dog is gone a little extra long the next morning? It will be hard to know whether the dog is having trouble opening the door or whether he's finishing off the potato chips. At what point would you fuss at him and tell him to leave the chips alone? Who knows! You cannot see what he's doing. The moment you choose to fuss might be the very moment he finally took hold of the strap to open the door.

A trainer and a client have many options on how to beat such circumstances. Creative training can provide methods to make the dog believe that you *can* see him. Or that something in the environment will "correct" him if he doesn't do what's expected. Choosing an appropriate breed can help a lot with certain jobs. Starting with a pup and carefully controlling the circumstances in which he grows up and learns "life's lessons" can be a powerful factor. You can predispose him to think that certain dilemmas are favorably solved by certain actions. But these are all training discussions, and not necessarily best addressed here.

Canine Initiative

I could go on for some time of stories about dogs who applied initiative to their training and provided wonderful results to their owners. One such client had a very reliable hearing assistance dog (a small Lab mix) who began seriously "acting up" one night. She refused to allow her owner to sleep. Pawed at the kitchen door, but would not go outside. Scratched at the kitchen floor, and wouldn't come when called. Refused to stay on her bed. Paced and fussed and made a general nuisance of herself. After checking every alarm and noise-making apparatus in the house multiple times, the frustrated owner finally—very apologetically—used a TDY service to call the fire department and ask if someone could possibly come and double-check her house. She wondered if there might be some kind of a short or something making noise, but no smoke reaching the smoke detectors. The firemen came, but found no fire, no short. What they did find was an intruder in the unfinished basement, evidently looking for a way into the house. The dog had never been in the basement. Had never been taught to listen for man-made sounds. Had never been encouraged to be protective. Yet something was out of order, she knew it, and did everything she could to "alert" her owner.

Realistic Views

Unfortunately, there is no means of establishing a scientific basis for determining what percentage of such incidents result from good training versus good dogs. My opinion is that you have to have both. A good dog can sense when you are injured or when something is out of kilter from normal. That is completely normal pack psychology for any dog, regardless of training. A good dog is likely to notice these things quickly. But unlike pack circumstances in the wild, a potential "threat" from an illness, for instance, would be vague to the dog and not understood. There are no predators to battle, no non-pack-members to chase away. So the dog needs to look for other solutions to reduce the tension he finds himself experiencing. Good training might very well predispose that good dog to see if a known behavior will bring its normal praise from his pack leader, thereby reducing the tension and adjusting his uncomfortable situation to one he likes better. In the process of recognizing a seizure, the dog has already been taught the response. In some way unknown to us, the onset of the seizure is noticeable to him—he's been aware of it probably every time it happened. Now he's just anticipating the rest of the sequence.

However, despite any amazing story you ever read about a service dog reminding you to mail the utility payments, don't deceive yourself into thinking you're watching Lassie reruns. This is a dog, and he is bound by concepts a dog understands. In fairness to yourself, the dog, and the trainer, understand from the outset that some tasks for a service dog simply cannot ever be guaranteed the same way as whether or not a dog will sit when you give the command. The nature of the tasks simply do not allow for situation control and repetitions necessary for training.

TASK SORTING

So, finally, returning to our original question: what can a dog realistically be trained to do? What can you count on? To give yourself a starting point, stick with the specific and the concrete. Write out a list of tasks you would expect of the dog, just as you did with the "examples" at the beginning of the chapter. Then with the help of the Yes/No questions, divide your list of tasks into three categories.

Category 1: Observable Tasks
Tasks for which specific training can be done with all variables available and controlled.

Category 2: Non-Observable Tasks
Tasks for which specific training can be done, but the dog will be acting out of your line of sight and/or direct control.

Category 3: Non-Reinforceable Tasks
Tasks for which you cannot control or recreate the variables at will, or in which the handler is not physically capable of reinforcement.

Look long and hard at Category 1, the tasks that can be directly observed and reinforced. I would advise most clients to decide based on whether or not they consider those tasks, by themselves, worth the effort and expense of obtaining a dog.

For decisions still hanging in the balance, I would suggest factoring in Category 2. These are often very teachable tasks, but may be quite time-and effort-intensive with less-than-perfect results.

Category 3 is a law unto itself. It's a hopeless dichotomy that some of the most critically important service dog tasks have to land on this list—seizure alert being only one example. Just one single Category 3 task might be a client's entire reason for wanting a service dog. That's okay. If the effort and possibility of a good outcome is acceptable to you—pick the best trainer with the best track record you can find, and proceed! But always keep in mind the less concrete nature of what you're attempting. Canine jobs in this category should be sufficiently important to you—in terms of expended time and money—to attempt when there are no guarantees. If not, don't consider these tasks anything but gravy for your main objective.

CHOOSE CAREFULLY

Most well-established service dog training programs are well aware of such distinctions. If it is your intention to use such a program, I present this chapter only to help you understand and apply your efforts to the training process. If you are proceeding on your own and planning to negotiate with a private trainer, this is an incredibly important part of your decision. Make sure you choose a trainer who understands the differences and doesn't promise you the moon for pennies—or for thousands.

Worst-Case Scenario

Coping with one disability presents enough challenges. Coping with two completely unrelated disabilities gets mind boggling. Stephanie had one of the most complex situations I'd ever encountered. Born with cerebral palsy, Stephanie was no stranger to finding creative solutions. A refusal to take 'no' for an answer had seen her through high school and college, the successful start of a home business, and the birth of her daughter. At 34 years of age, life changed again when she was diagnosed with multiple sclerosis. Prognoses were grim. Doctors were unencouraging.

With a fierce determination, Stephanie pursued new strategies. Research about service dogs brought her to my door, and it quickly became apparent that her most critical need was a dog to provide a safety net by giving an alarm or fetching a phone if she got into trouble.

A beautiful dark-red Golden Retriever, Kelly, was selected for the job. Training began. Several times during this process (which was one of my earliest experiences in attempting to get a dog to generalize a phone retrieve into extremely varied circumstances) I worried that acquaintances might institutionalize me before I finished the job. One day a friend stopped by. As she knocked on my front door, she belatedly became aware I was already nearby—upside down in the corner of the front porch, mostly concealed behind a large potted plant.

"Are you drunk or sick or meditating?" my friend directed her skeptical question to my feet—all that was visible.

"None of the above," I answered. "I'm trying to figure out what position a person would be in if they fell back here."

"What? No fall? You got back there on purpose?" Clearly she thought I needed professional help. "What ails you, chick?"

Nothing ailed me. Kelly's training was currently a matter of dreaming up new and bizarre places and positions from which I would ask him to retrieve the cordless phone. A parlor trick is one matter, when you have chances to repeat commands and ensure that your friends are properly impressed with your clever dog. Relying on the dog potentially to save your neck is another scenario entirely. When Kelly finally transferred to Stephanie's house, the gradually-varied routine began all over again. This time it was even harder, as Stephanie had to work around her limitations to simulate falls for Kelly's training—and her own training. But she persevered; she knew her safety might be at stake.

Stephanie worked for months to establish a correct understanding with Kelly about the phone command. It became a matter of routine, and they practiced it almost without thinking anymore. Even though her in-home training phase was long finished, she continued to use the function daily to ensure his proper response to the cue. Stephanie had a few tumbles here and there, which was unfortunately normal for her, but only once did she have to use the "phone" command to call her husband for help. The other times, she was always able (with Kelly's help) to get herself up and going again.

However, real life final exams have a way of surpassing our expectations of "worst-case scenario." When the true test arrived for Kelly, it was far more serious than anything that had ever happened before. Stephanie was moving around the kitchen. In attempts to hurry, she tripped There was no time to break her fall or otherwise protect herself. As she fell, Stephanie's head struck the corner of a cabinet—with great force.

As consciousness slowly returned, Stephanie was aware she was badly injured, but she wasn't sure even exactly what had happened. Her vision was clouded and dark. She was having trouble making her voice work at all. Though she didn't know it, Stephanie had a severe concussion and a fractured skull, including intercranial bleeding. Before the day was over, she would be undergoing emergency surgery to relieve pressure on her brain. But as she lay there, crumpled against the kitchen counter, her only coherent thought was to somehow get the words organized and uttered to call her dog. She knew he could bring her the phone. All the bottom-numeral speed dial keys on the cordless unit were set to 911. As Stephanie exhaled a deep breath and summoned energy for the effort, she became aware of a slight breeze near her arm. It was Kelly's tail fanning the air. A hard, cool object pressed against her hand. Kelly was already there—with the phone.

———◆❖◆———

CHAPTER 7: THE JOB DESCRIPTION

SUGGESTED READING

Minimum Standards for Service Dogs, Revision 2. Renton, WA: Delta Society. 2002. This booklet is available for purchase or for free download in PDF from *www.deltasociety.org*.

Chapter 8:

Service Dogs and Children

The decision for anyone to use a service dog is a complex one, but it becomes even more so when the question is regarding a minor. Successful implementation of a service dog with a child has even more hurdles and hoops than the same dog doing similar work for an adult. Before anyone jumps to conclusions, know that I would be the last person to criticize the idea of a functional child/service dog team. Critical? No! Wary? You bet! Please bear with me and think this through. Just as many aspects of general dog training intensify when one extends them to service dogs, so the entire discussion intensifies yet again with the concept of a child handling a dog in public settings. You, the adult, the parent, the caregiver, are responsible for your child—and by extension your child's handling of the dog if you allow him to do so without you present. You are responsible practically, intellectually, and legally, and those are hefty considerations.

PROS AND CONS

Almost everyone has read or heard stories of children's lives being revolutionized by service dogs. When it happens, words are completely inadequate to describe the success. Again, I stress that when everything is workable, advisable, and safe, I'll be the first to organize the cheering squad. But the percentage of situations meeting that criteria is almost certainly lower than many people think. A service dog is a tool, not a piece of magic. A successful working relationship is a huge amount of hard work; a service dog is no more correct for every child than would be the identical wheelchair or writing device.

Before we delve into specifics, consider something from the flip side of the same coin. The number of children with disabilities who could benefit from a trained *companion* dog, for in-home use only, is probably *higher* than most people think. We briefly referred to companion dogs in Chapter 2 when defining terms. Companion dogs are, like service dogs, specifically trained to assist a disabled person with various tasks. Companion dogs, however, unlike service dogs, are not intended for work in public settings.

ADOLESCENCE MAGNIFIED

Learning to use a service dog is no small task for a mature, responsible adult with normal amounts of self-discipline. For those of us who might have forgotten the intensity of peer pressure, frustration, and general harassment associated with adolescence, allow me to remind you about it now. Regardless of what jobs the dog does or does not perform for a child, the moment you turn your son or daughter loose in public with a service dog, you've immediately accomplished several things. You've raised his profile among his peers and made him different from others in a way that's guaranteed to attract attention. You've given him extra responsibility. You've increased his physical vulnerability to teasing and abuse, since others now have the dog as a target as well as the child himself. You've complicated a daily routine into one that involves caring for a dog.

You've put him in a position where his successes and failures with the dog are readily observable to his peers.

Can all of this turn out well? Will the peer group respond with admiration for his skill? Adoration for the dog? Help or cooperation when needed? Respect for his requests not to interfere? Increased desire to interact and be friends with the dog's handler? They might. Make no mistake—it does happen. When everything goes well, a service dog can increase a child's independence and functionality, plus be the biggest morale boost he's ever known. This dog just turned him into something new—a pretty darn good dog handler/trainer—and he's better at that skill than almost everyone else around him. Such a success can play a major role in turning a child's difficult world right side up. But be careful betting the farm on such an outcome. Things might turn out otherwise.

Dogs attending school with young owners have presented me with some of the most formidable training challenges of my career. I've never lost hope because the success stories *do* happen—and they chill you and thrill you all at once. However, I consider it fair to say that for the majority of young clients I've worked with, the results have been a trade-off of benefits for frustration. A few have been epic-scale disasters. At the worst extremes, I've seen service dogs (in high schools especially) subjected to actual physical abuse by other students, teased to the point of ruining their entire effectiveness for work, and provoked to snapping. I've seen more than a few kids who simply could not resist the desire to show off, comply with nonsense, endanger themselves, or otherwise misuse the presence of the dog. In the ultimately worst situation I ever encountered, one dog was taken forcefully from her owner (while the teenager went hysterical), shaved half bald in one of the school's locker rooms, then locked in a cupboard in an unused wing. It was several hours before trainers, school staff, and the police located the dog, by which time she had broken three teeth and ripped open several pads on her paws trying to escape the closet. Penalty to the students involved? One week of detention. Vet bill to the child's parents? Close to $2,000. Trauma to the child and dog? Enormous.

"Things I Like and Don't Like"

"Lots of different people ask me what it's like to have an assistance dog in high school. That's a hard question to answer because there are different ways to answer. Luke is my assistance dog, and he is a Labrador mix. We started training together between my sophomore and junior years of high school because I needed help getting to the bus stop and also to my job. The way things worked, he had to go to school with me, even though that was really pretty hard to do. Even though he helped me a lot during school, like picking up things for me so I didn't have to ask for help, it was a lot of work to take care of him, too. Lots of times I didn't get to spend lunchtime with my friends because I had to take Luke outside and then pick up after him, which takes me quite a lot of time.

"There are things I like and don't like about working with Luke. I don't like everybody staring at him (and at me) all the time. It can be kind of embarrassing. I didn't like that I sometimes couldn't have fun with other people the way I used to because many of them don't understand about dogs and that they don't like to be teased. If you can't put up with guys teasing you, then they just have more fun. But if they're teasing your dog, then you have to find a way to make them stop for real, and that's pretty hard. But having Luke was good for me because I want to go to college. If I didn't have him, there would be mornings that I wouldn't be able to get to school because there wasn't anybody to help. And if I want to go to college, I needed to start working. I got a job in an office answering phones every afternoon, but I had to have Luke's help to get there. Maybe I can get a scholarship, but I'll still have to keep a job. Without Luke I don't think I would be able to go. I hope Luke will get a degree too, if I graduate. He works very hard and I think he will have earned it by then."

—*Contributed by Laura Miles, written in 1997. Laura recently completed her Masters Degree in Sociology and has entered a career in education. Luke accompanied her across the platform as she received her degree.*

PACK ORDER

Dogs are "pack" creatures, rather than natural loners. In a wild state, this pack is made up of various canines of various ages and gender. In the domestic state, dogs' pack is made up of all the people and other species with whom they reside. They define social order, responsibilities, and even reproductive rights according to who leads this pack and who makes up the various members. This is an interesting concept when one considers the subject of liability, as discussed in Chapter 6 about a service dog's potential interactions with others in public, and think for a few moments about whether or not you can trust entire control of a dog to a child. Again, all the normal issues are more complicated when the dog is being handled by a child instead of an adult. One of the largest of those considerations is a dog's natural characteristic to be protective of the "young" in his pack.

Children Are "Puppies"

Most dogs have a pretty good sense of "pack order." Once incorporated into a home, it's not difficult for them to figure out who the leaders and protectors are. In the dog's mind, the next logical step is that children are the "pups" of the pack, and it's automatically his job to help protect. This is hardwired for the species. You can moderate it to some extent, but don't fool yourself that you're going to erase it completely. If the pack leader is temporarily out of the picture, the dog is even more likely to perceive or interpret something (perhaps even an otherwise-normal something) as a threat to the child. As covered more extensively later, the body language and circumstances of a disabled person—perhaps especially a child—are often what a dog might consider vulnerable. Coping with the dog's perception calls for training, judgment, and unfailing vigilance. If the handler is not paying careful attention, he could easily miss a cue that the dog feels concern about a bystander's actions. If the handler's training has been inadequate, he might not even recognize such cues. Consequently, it's not all that hard, over a period of time and repeatedly missed cues, for a snap or bite to happen. A parent had better be very sure of the child's reliability and training.

Follow The Leader
Another dilemma is the dog's choice of person with whom he wants to bond. A lot of dogs—quite a few of them being sociable, easy-going, eager-to-please types (typical service dog personality)—are inclined to bond most strongly with the authority figure in the home. Whether a service dog or companion dog is desired, parents must understand this is not a dog who is going to fulfill the role of a family pet. Specific concerns and technique are best addressed by a trainer for each individual situation, but remember that all adults in the family may have to work hard in denying the dog the bond to which he might naturally gravitate. The dog has to learn to see the child as the primary focus.

PARENTAL CONSIDERATIONS
If you believe a service dog or companion dog is right for your child, there are several factors I'd urge you to consider before finalizing a decision.

Whose Project?
First, make sure the desire is actually your child's and not your own. You (rather like me) may be of the mindset that thinks "Who in the world would NOT want to do this?" Your child might view the matter differently, however, and for any variety of reasons, including a normal desire to please, be reluctant to tell you so. I have, unfortunately, seen more than one situation where thousands of dollars and hundreds of hours were expended (with miserable

results) before a youngster dared to confide to me, "I really don't *want* a dog, but I don't want to tell my parents...."

Balance

Second, determine—very specifically—which functions your child actually needs help to perform, keeping in mind that it is *additional* work to take care of the needs of a service dog in public. Make sure the objective justifies the process. There are many ways to view this dilemma. Very few seriously disabled children spend much time outside the supervision of an adult—especially not while in school. On one hand, it is true that there is satisfaction and increased independence from each task a child can accomplish for himself—or via his dog—without having to ask for help. On the other hand, depending on the nature of the disability, the extra time needed to interact with the dog and the distraction of doing so might seriously hinder the child's educational program. This is a highly individualized decision that only a parent, working closely with professional educators, can make.

Dependability

Next: forget the disability for a moment and give some consideration to the individual maturity level of your child. Physical limitations aside, if you could not be comfortable having the child alone in public *without* the dog—in terms of trustworthiness and correct behavior—then there's no way it's going to work *with* the dog. However, if your child works an after-school job or is otherwise regularly outside the home for a specific purpose, such as using public transportation, receiving tutoring, or attending extracurricular activities, you may want to give the concept of a service dog some serious thought. A well-trained dog could very well give him the edge needed to excel.

Outside Help

Finally, in all cases I would encourage parents to seek the opinions of at least the following people before reaching a decision: the child's teacher(s), the school administrator, your child's physician, and any therapists (physical, speech, occupational, etc.) with whom he works. Though perhaps not practical for everyone, I would strongly encourage you to consider some professional counseling if at all possible. This is not because anything is "wrong" with your family; it is merely be an effort to add objectivity and an outside perspective to the decision-making process—which can get pretty complicated with multiple people! You might be able to find a local therapist (perhaps even the guidance counselor from your child's school) who is a "dog person" himself and would have a better understanding of what you're discussing.

Some programs have begun providing training about service dogs to a state-licensed counselor or social worker, and in turn, recommending that counselor (or possibly even covering the costs) to prospective clients. As I look back on the years since 1998 when we incorporated this practice at Dogs for Disabled, I consider it some of the best money we ever spent. It wasn't too many years before we invited the counselor onto our board of directors to help maintain perspective and accurate communication. I would heartily recommend similar counseling to any family who can make the arrangements.

Companion Dogs

If the concept of service dogs working for children is sometimes over-romanticized, the practice of companion dogs working for children is very often *under*-emphasized. I am vociferously in favor in companion dogs for kids and would like to see a whole lot more of them in place. In almost any circumstances where it is desirable to the child and feasible for the parents, the potential is huge. The work with the dog promotes responsibility, increased situational awareness, and development of better abilities to interact with others. Furthermore, the companionship issue itself should not be underestimated. This is at least as much of a factor for children as for adults! Finally, the skills built in handling a companion dog will provide an excellent basis for the child to transition to an actual service dog later, if he so chooses.

That said, even a companion dog in the home will be a lot of work for a child to learn to use correctly. Be sure that you, as a parent, are not considering the dog to be a quick-fix for every challenge against which your child struggles. While you may recognize that fact in your head, make sure your emotions and even your cautious expectations agree. The benefits for your child, in maturity, independence, and self-confidence, could be almost incalculable. But the project will be work—a whole lot of work. Not only for the child, but for you, too. If you're looking for solutions to reduce work load and reduce complications, a dog is not the answer. It would be more accurate to consider the dog as an additional project you would "sign up for" just like you'd enroll your child in karate, ballet, or music.

Some years ago I had a parent with two children, both of whom had spina bifida, request two companion dogs, one for each child. It so happened that this lady home-schooled her children, and the dogs became the practice laboratory for a whole new project involving science, sociology, health, physical education, and computer research. The kids took working field trips to the vet, to the park, to the local pet shops, to kennels, and to dog shows. Every trip involved study preparation, homework, grades, and potential rewards. I was beyond impressed—I was floored. By the end of the school year, those kids could paralyze the average dog professional with the information they'd spout, and they had better control of their dogs than most adults I know.

The older of the two is now in college—absolutely sailing through a pre-vet program—and has a beautifully-performing service dog towing her around campus. The training process for "placing" her new service dog was essentially limited to telling her the dog's name and ensuring she knew the right command words. She didn't much need my help with anything else.

Siblings

Last in the lineup of specific considerations, if you have other children, have a plan in mind for how they might react to either a service dog or companion dog. Jealousy? A desire to participate or for a dog of their own? If so, can that be accommodated? Or diverted to another pastime of their choice? Only you can decide what is appropriate to answer these concerns, but as previously stressed, if you want this dog to work effectively for the child with the disability, then handling, care, and training of the dog cannot be a community project.

TECHNICALITIES

If you've been paying close attention, a rather sticky point may have occurred to you. The definition of a service animal may have sparked your realization that a companion dog meets the legal definition of a service animal. Once a dog has received specific and individualized training to assist with a person's disability, he is, indeed, technically a service dog. The "companion dog" term (or possibly a different term: social dog, personal therapy dog, helper dog) originates with the trainer or the program. The term has nothing to do with the law. While normally a program's contract will specifically prohibit the use of a companion dog in a public setting, it is also true that such a prohibition is a matter between you and the program, enforceable only so far as the terms of the contract are legally enforceable. Therefore, can you take a companion dog in public? Until the law changes, yes you can. However, until the general nature of people and dogs both change...*please don't!*

Remember that if you defy the requirements of a program or trainer, you are probably negating their support—and also their shared liability if something should happen. (Depending on the terms of your agreement with them, you may be legally required to surrender the dog if they insist.) You're also very likely going to screw up a perfectly good dog who hasn't been properly introduced to the distractions of working in a public setting. Most important, you're putting your child and others at risk, again because the dog has probably not been adequately trained to ignore the distractions he will face in public.

TAKE YOUR TIME

Any parent can confirm that the delicate art of rearing children, all by itself, is a highly individualized affair. Add a disability here and there, and then toss in the complexity of dog behavior, and you have a rather complicated set of factors to work through. You are in charge. You are in the home. You know what is happening there better than anyone else. I can merely offer factors for you to consider. It's not much comfort, I'm sure, to point out that ultimately you will be responsible to both the child and the dog for the decision you make. The only directive I can give that applies to 100% of cases is this: take your time. Don't rush any decision until you're completely comfortable you've thought it all the way through and obtained all the professional advice available.

If you choose to incorporate a service dog into your child's school and/or work routine, review the following, remembering that school personnel are not responsible to provide care for the dog. Make sure you have solutions for:

- Available time and an established location for the dog to relieve himself

- Means available for the child to provide the dog with frequent access to water.
- An established protocol for your child to contact you in case of a medical emergency for the dog.
- Alternate transportation available that can accommodate the dog if your child's normal means is interrupted for any reason
- The dog's equipment (possibly containing metal) does not violate any applicable safety standards of the school.
- Your child knows who within the school to contact, and how, if anyone interferes with or harms his dog.
- What and how your homeowner's insurance coverage would apply to any damage or liability resulting from the use of the dog in a school.

SUGGESTED READING

"Service Dogs for Children with Disabilities: When are they the right prescription?" This article was originally published in *Alert* magazine. See *www.deltasociety.org/nsdc/alertv06n03.btm*

Chapter 9:

Breeds

Few people who like dogs fail to have a favorite breed. Many people have a strong preference for a particular breed because of a dog they saw or else because they have a already have a concept about what breed a service dog should be. Many breeders who are thinking of donating or selling to service dog agencies have a collection of reasons they believe their own breed is best for the job. Frankly, even most trainers have a predisposition to choose a certain breed, often simply because they have the greatest knowledge of a certain breed. However, any kind of generalization is a poor start for evaluating breed selection. Asking "which breed is best for service dog work?" is comparable to asking "which vehicle is best to drive." To either question, the only truly logical response is: "For *what?*"

Breed traits and subsequent selection is a fascinating subject to me—a common topic over many an extensive dinner with trainer and breeder buddies. When it comes to choosing a service dog, however, it's time to put personal preferences aside and take a close, objective look at what best suits the situation. The sheer volume of informative books, tapes, and web sites on varying breeds is dizzying to contemplate, much less wade through. This brief discussion cannot possibly replace the information many breeders and specialists have spent decades collecting and formatting. No one person can be an expert on all breeds. However, I want to try to hit some highlights and give you a starting place for exploration.

PERSONALITY

First, let's narrow down the discussion. Though discussing breed variation has overlap with discussing temperament, the two topics are not the same. Every breed has variation of temperament among its own individuals. More and less dominant individuals are found within each breed, also more and less confident dogs, more and less independent dogs. True, some breeds have one or more of these characteristics as a typical strength, but to make the mistake of generalizing is to invite trouble. Retriever breeds are a great example. Many assume that because retrievers normally greet total strangers with enthusiasm that they are "always friendly" and "don't bite." *Any* dog can bite!

TEMPERAMENT WITHIN PERSONALITY

Whether discussing the friendliness of retrievers or the independence of terriers, guard yourself from generalizations. Certain breeds have certain "interests," per se, but if you put a pack together of the same breed with all members having the same interest (whether trailing the rabbits or chasing the sheep) some members would still emerge as dominant and pushy, whereas others would be subservient and agreeable. Some would be nervous about new environments, others bold. That's temperament. However, among a pack of beagles, I'll bet you a buck that every single one of them, regardless of temperament, will scent and follow a rabbit that crosses their trail. And almost all Border Collies will intensely watch, and probably chase, sheep. That's breed inclination—or personality.

Therefore, when we start trying to sort out breed variations, we are looking for the average interests and tendencies of the breed. The practical inclinations. Think of it this way: what would any particular dog choose to do for fun? Run around and smell things? Look for something to chase? Or pick up a toy and parade proudly about?

TRAINER RATIONALE

If you are working through an established program or experienced trainer, it's almost certainly best just to leave the entire matter of breed selection up to them. Many programs—perhaps most—insist on this. Programs, especially those dependent on outside contributions for funding, must make these decisions based not only on what is possible, but what is practical. They need to use the most effective, most timely solution per dollar. That is automatically going to limit exploration of dogs or breeds that are merely "possible" and stick with proven formulas. Some of them will be working with dogs exclusively from within their own breeding stock, so as to reduce unknowns and increase the predictability of their finished product.

Long ago I stopped trying to count the number of phone calls from prospective clients who wanted a service dog, but insisted their service dog be a certain breed. As the years rolled on, I learned to sort out this situation with a hypothetical question. "If I told you that it would not be possible to train your favorite breed as your service dog, are you still interested in learning more?" If the caller's answer was "no," I would wish them heartfelt good luck and suggest they check with another program or trainer. If they were willing at least to spend time thinking it through, I knew it was more likely we would get somewhere. If there was a way to accommodate their preference, with reasonable expectations about the result, I would usually investigate. But not always. In fact, there were certain breeds I would not consider using. And you are likely to encounter the same among the trainers and programs you interview.

While you may view such policies as bias, understand that such policies—or even just preferences—may have mostly to do with a trainer's experience in selecting good temperaments from within a given breed. And if you miss every other point about breeds, please note that experience is nothing to be sneezed at! *It takes much time and effort to learn about a breed.* It takes time to learn their variations, their habits, and the traits of certain genetic families within the breed. If a trainer doesn't have much experience with a particular breed, he'd be out of his mind just to sashay out and pick a sample by guesswork. If a trainer doesn't have access to an experienced breeder who can provide guidance, he'd be far better off to leave it alone and use something he knows well enough to predict.

RESEARCH

If you, as a prospective user of a service dog, are choosing your own dog, the very first thing I would encourage you to do is read some books. The second is to contact some reputable breeders and find out what they think of your plan. Furthermore, plan to contact more than one breeder—preferably not less than half a dozen. You are looking for a consensus, not individual opinion. Beyond that, by "reputable," I mean breeders who screen breeding stock for genetic defects, interview buyers with extreme thoroughness, keep track of their puppies after sale, and are willing to take back their sale dogs who later become unwanted pets. In other words, *don't* choose the breeder who advertises on a web site that "all you have to do is give them a ring, having your Visa or Mastercard handy."

The American Kennel Club's web site on breeder education can give you a starting place for developing your criteria.[1]

I would also recommend that you find a breeder who routinely screens dogs for performance capability as well as for genetic soundness and correct conformation. All three are important. Just exactly what performance capability might be sought in a particular dog depends on the breed. Whether performance is a matter of herding, hunting, retrieving, scenting, or going to ground after "varmints," dogs who have been selected for performance ability as well as physical structure are likely to score higher in both trainability and health. I'd also score extra points for any breeder who routinely titles his breeding stock in the obedience or agility rings. Above all, please do not rush off to the local pet store or flea market and pick out a pup of your desired breed. Such dogs are almost always the products either of "puppy mills" and/or extremely careless breeding practices. Reputable breeders simply do not sell their puppies in such a manner. To buy a dog through those forums is begging to be fleeced of your purchase price and future expectations.

PREDISPOSITIONS

Why are dog breeds different and why does it matter?

History

All our modern breeds are the same species, *canis familiaris*, almost all of which originated in the same genetics. The current differences we observe among breeds are a matter of selective breeding over a many generations. The varied results are easily visible in the physical differences. What we need to keep in mind is that the *mental* differences in these breeds are usually every bit

---

[1] See "Responsible Breeding Steps" at *www.akc.org/breeders/resp_breeding/index.cfm.*

as pronounced as the physical ones, especially in the cases of dogs who were developed to perform a specific working function. The various long-ago founders of breeds were pretty ruthless in their selection of dogs. Everything was based on the dogs' ability and desire to perform a job. In many (dare I say most) cases, the physical appearance of the dog happened as a secondary result, proving the correctness of the old breeders' saying: "form follows function." In most real canine working jobs, looks were just gravy. The breeders chose the dog because he was capable and interested and willing to do a certain job. As a handful of various such dogs were crossed and re-crossed, a type of appearance emerged, eventually becoming the dominant appearance.

Assumptions

Today we have people who swoon at the gorgeous appearance of some breeds (and indeed many of them are tremendously beautiful) and/or their amazingly intense response to breed-specific training…then think because the dog is beautiful and smart he will love them enough to turn into the perfect couch potato for their tiny Manhattan apartment. Six months later, the owner is furious and disgusted, the house is destroyed, and the dog is psychotic with general frustration. News flash: there's probably not a single thing wrong with the dog. He's just being what he was developed to be. Such situations are entirely the fault of people—both the owners who chose the dog and the errant breeder who agreed to the sale. Before you go dog shopping, hang a card around your neck with this comment written on it: "Remind me that different breeds *think* as differently as they *look*."

As with almost all our topics, if any principle applies to dogs in general, the application intensifies in service dogs. If you're about to spend multiple thousands on a dog, training, and equipment, you need to take an extremely careful look at your home, your lifestyle, and circumstances to determine what breed will best fit in and meet your need. Breed considerations go beyond the way a dog thinks. You'll have much to consider, such as the amount of coat, whether or not the dog drools a lot, or even just the size.

SIZE
Size is an especially important consideration. Take a few moments to think about the following size factors as you think about choosing a breed.

Functionality
Any dog you choose must be physically capable of performing the job you have in mind. If the job includes pulling a wheelchair, the dog will need to be sufficiently large and strong to pull the chair with your weight in it. If the job includes providing balance while walking, the dog needs to be the correct height and physical construction to wear a harness that puts a handle in reasonable proximity to your normal hand position.

Fit
Despite needing a certain amount of muscle power or height, bigger is not always better. In fact, quite the reverse. Consider what you might face in trying to stow a 130-lb dog under a restaurant table, or worse yet, in aircraft seating. Any experienced service dog trainer will start getting uneasy about public accommodation when a prospective dog's weight goes over 90 pounds. My personal rule of thumb on these matters is to choose the smallest available dog that is physically capable of the job. If two dogs are equal in all other ways, I'll choose the one that weighs 70 pounds over the one that weighs 80. Ease of public accommodation is certainly one factor, and that includes the city bus, a taxi cab, a client's own

vehicle, the "cubicle" work space so common in modern offices, theater seating, and many other locations.

Expense

However slight might be the differences, they do add up over the lifetime of the dog. A smaller dog eats less, requires smaller (and less expensive) equipment such as crates and harnesses, costs less to groom, and even his medications and/or preventatives (such as those for fleas, ticks, and heartworm) are cheaper.

Longevity

Smaller dogs typically live longer than larger dogs. At the extreme ends of this dilemma are the giant breeds, many of which are considered geriatric by five or six years of age. Given the amount of training and expense a client puts into the acquisition of a service dog, even a year or two's difference in working life is no small matter.

Health

While genetic diseases and health problems plague dogs of every size and almost every breed, certain ones are limited, or at least eased, by smaller size. Highest on that list are structural issues such as degenerative or arthritic joints. Service dogs spend a large portion of their lives working on hard surfaces: concrete floors, sidewalks, streets, and parking lots. Less bulk means less impact and generally less wear and tear. Small size doesn't guarantee freedom from problems, but it probably will lessen the effects. If two seven-year-old dogs crop up with arthritis in a foot or leg (whether genetically based or possibly due to a fall or other injury), the one who weighs 85 pounds is highly likely to have more trouble than the one weighing 60.

MINDSET

Moving from physical to mental, let's consider some basics about canine personality. As already emphasized, whatever breed you are considering was probably developed for a certain purpose—even if the purpose was to sit on laps and look cute. Your first step in evaluating is to identify that purpose. Then you'll need to consider how well the purpose might fit in with your needs and the job you want this dog to perform. If I tried to explore them all, this book would be too big to carry, but let's go over a few examples about some of the more common issues.

Retrievers

Goldens and Labradors, with a few Flat Coats thrown in, are undoubtedly the most frequently-used service dog in the United States. It's my personal opinion that most clients who need a typical assistance dog for common tasks will do best with some type of retriever. Many trainers agree, though various ones will give different reasons. The list of characteristics that favor retrievers is long, but one of the top entries is the function that gives them their name. The developers of the breed had little patience with a dog that wasn't naturally inclined to pick up and carry things. As the Dogs for Disabled training director has said many times, "these dogs normally come out of the womb saying 'everything goes in my mouth.'" If you have a job for a dog that includes a great number of mouth-oriented tasks, you'll want to consider a dog who is naturally inclined to fetch and carry. All of its working career, you'll be telling the dog, "pick it up." "Hold that." "Pull on this." "Carry that." It's much more pleasant for everyone if you're using a dog to whom these behaviors come naturally. When attempting to solve a problem, retrievers will generally default to something "mouth oriented."

Furthermore, since retrievers' original selection had nothing to do with guarding, most of them lack the natural aloofness and/or suspicion common in breeds developed to protect. Most of them just basically like people, which makes them easy to take in public. This trait also makes it easier to transfer their bond from the trainer to the client—often a huge consideration! Conversely, let's suppose your situation is one where the amount of "people distraction" will be enormous. Because of your circumstances (for instance, a busy, crowded office when your employment time is spent primarily on the phone) you might have limited ability to correct the dog. Therefore you may be better suited by a breed less inclined to greet every stranger with a wagging tail and a face-wash.

On the less positive side, retrievers can be very physically insensitive, which is also a result of the original selection criteria. Breeders were looking for dogs that would charge through brambles, briars, ice floes, tough brush, rocks, and very cold water to get their jaws on an elusive duck. The dog that said "OUCH" and quit the game at the first slap of a passing twig was immediately weeded out. Over many generations, this has tended to create some dogs you would swear have no nerve endings within three inches of any skin surface. Some Labradors can remodel any door frame in your house and hardly notice; how much less would he notice his passing impact on your leg— even if it just put you on the floor. He's not being a bad dog; he's just being a Lab. Such issues are ones where input from an experienced breeder is invaluable. They know the genetic lines of their breed and can help you select to minimize such issues.

Guarding Breeds

Most breeds that fit under this heading are popular ones from two groups the American Kennel Club calls "Working Breeds" and

"Herding Breeds." I am grouping dogs from those two categories together and referring to them as "Guarding Breeds" because a noteworthy portion of their original purpose was to protect property, people, or livestock against predators, human vandals, and possibly even natural events. My self-constructed heading of guarding breeds would include dogs such as Doberman Pinschers, Rottweilers, Boxers, Giant Schnauzers, German Shepherds, Belgian Malinois, Bouviers, and quite a few more. While many guarding breeds have sagacious and steady personalities, are very biddable, and very willing to work for their owners, you should keep in mind that these dogs were *intended* to be suspicious of strangers and newcomers. Careful input from a good breeder and a good trainer can help you decide if this type of dog is right for you. However, you must be aware that you are automatically taking on a greater responsibility than with a dog of less protective tendencies. You must take extra care never to allow a non-threatening situation to be misinterpreted by your dog.

Please take a careful look at what we are asking of dogs by becoming service dogs. You and your family and your dog make up the pack. Pack defense is an absolutely hard-wired genetic trait of all canines, regardless of breed. It's never entirely going away. If you have the notion that you can socialize or desensitize any dog completely beyond any possibility of a defensive bite, get over it. You will not.

Dogs use a body language system of communication that is entirely different from that of humans. For instance, think about what dogs do if they are stalking something. Even if it's a matter of a puppy "stalking" a toy in your living room, what are the preliminary actions to capturing his "prey?" Probably every person reading this book has seen a puppy stare at the toy and creep closer and closer before the big pounce. This isn't behavior you taught to a two or three-month old puppy. It happens because he's a dog. Obvious, yes? Great. But a dog's basic understanding of such stalking behavior might extend in some surprising ways.

Think for a moment about what might happen one day when you, a service dog user, arrives at a shopping mall with your dog. Your arrival is considerably less of an event than it was 10 years ago, since people are more accustomed to seeing dogs working in that role. But a service dog is still enough of a curiosity—or perhaps just a subject of fascination to some—to draw lots of attention. Very often people who are interested in or impressed by your dog (or maybe even frightened) will stop what they are doing and…STARE. They might not bother you, or speak, but watch they will. What do you suppose your dog (who stalks toys) thinks when half the nearby people stop moving and start looking …all straight at you? Some of these (kind and interested) people might even start inching closer for a better look at the gorgeous dog—still staring! If you are using a wheelchair, you're probably in a lower posture than most of the people around you, which is another measure of vulnerability in a dog's mind. If you're at all uneasy, whether about your dog's performance, about the amount of attention you're attracting, or maybe just because you're going to a job interview or are late for work, your dog is likely to notice. Some of these elements could cause a dog to believe there is a threat to you. Manageable? Yes. But it calls for correct and extensive training—especially if you're using a breed who is naturally inclined to protect.

Any service dog user should learn to read a dog's body language well enough to recognize when the dog is in the initial stages of concern or alert (long before a bite would happen). If you choose a guarding breed for your service dog, know from the outset that you may have to put a larger amount of work into both training and maintenance to get the same results you would get with a different dog.

Herding Breeds

Again, remember that several herding breeds, such as German Shepherds, Bouviers, and Malinois, were developed not only for herding, but for protection purposes as well. (Even Rottweilers were originally used for livestock control as well as guarding!) So there is considerable overlap between this category and guarding breeds. But in a "classic" herding dog such as the Border Collie, Australian Shepherd, or the Shetland Sheepdog, the tendency to pursue, guide, and control movement is definitely their dominating trait. Many of these dogs are absolutely, no-foolin' *going* to herd something, whether you consider it part of their job description or not. If you don't provide something to be herded, they'll choose something on their own. Passing cars. Your children. The neighbor's ducks or chickens. A butterfly. Or the stray cats hanging out behind the restaurant you just left. Can such dogs learn the technique of doing service work? Absolutely yes. These are some of the most trainable dogs in the world. But whether or not their actual personality is what you want is a matter for careful consideration and thorough input from an experienced breeder and trainer. Be practical and realistic. In short, if your next-door neighbors have a sheep farm, and you expect your service dog to do a large amount of off-leash and/or outdoor work, I'd think long and hard before choosing a Border Collie.

"Listen and Heed"

As mentioned in Chapter 1, a lot of errors in assistance dog training stem from a lack of information, rather than bad information. Here is a classic example of a time that my simply not knowing something led to a serious functional problem.

Several years ago, I paired a Border Collie mix with a man named Joe, who had Parkinson's disease. What I didn't understand (or at least didn't sufficiently apply to the context) was how tremendously visual some of these herding breeds are. To quote one of my long-time training friends, "You have to understand how much more these dogs see than average. They have to. You need them to see and respond to a sheep's eyelash flicker at 100 feet." Due to the nature of Parkinson's disease, this visually-oriented dog (who was otherwise essentially perfect in personality and training) went slap-flat out of his mind in less than a month because of all the "extra" visual cues he thought he was getting—which were nothing more than very normal Parkinson's tremors. Joe didn't understand. I didn't understand. To us, the tremors were actually pretty minor and not of much significance. He was able to make the larger gestures associated with commanding and controlling the dog just fine.

However, to the dog the tremors were hugely significant. He saw them as a constant source of stimulation and encouragement to do...something! But he wasn't sure exactly what. This wonderfully stable, biddable, willing dog was reduced to a perpetual state of anxiety, panting, and drooling. He could not relax, wouldn't hold stays, and often raced in circles when given a command, randomly offering one behavior after another faster than the client could possibly correct or reward. Once it dawned on me what was happening, the Border Collie mix was whisked away to a month or so of "vacation rehab." He was re-assigned to a young college student who was constantly on the go. Joe was much more successfully paired with a very unreactive, extremely easy-going Golden Retriever. Nothing was wrong with either dog. Both were extremely successful assistance dogs that are still working today. The first situation simply did not suit—a fact that I should have understood sooner...but learned.

Friends, talk to experienced, reputable breeders. Listen and heed!

Hunting Dogs

I include here both dogs that are searchers of game (pointers, setters) and dogs that are scenters of game (hounds). This group is another combination of dogs from the AKC's groups of "Sporting Breeds" and "Hounds." Both types have a natural tendency to notice and focus on game. Such inclinations can make them very challenging to deal with as a service animal. These inclinations have no connection with their temperament, per se, such as whether or not they are dominant toward people or manageable enough to handle. Those are separate issues. But the likelihood of such dogs being distracted by enticing scents or nearby wildlife (pigeons, squirrels, farm animals, rodents, or other pets) is extremely high. How big of an issue this is for you depends, as always, on your own situation. It may not be a problem at all. Or it may be huge. But be aware it's there and deserves consideration.

Some years ago I found a stray German Shorthaired Pointer who was not only one of the most beautiful dogs I've ever seen, but one of the most willing to work. I thought for sure I'd found the service dog candidate of the year. "Rosa" knocked down the first couple months of basic training with less effort than it takes to tell about it. Only when I began taking her into varied settings did the problem emerge. Let one stray fowl of pretty much any species cross her path, even at a distance, and Rosa would basically go into a standing coma. My chances of getting a nearby fence post to pay attention was higher than getting Rosa to do so. As long as that bird remained in her view, bribes, corrections, praise, or any other kind of pressure I could dream up got me absolutely nothing. The world started and stopped with the feathers in view.

Could I have leaned on her with enough corrections to push her into doing what I wanted? Yes, certainly. But the need for such extreme pressure does not bode well for the future client/service dog relationship. With regrets I handed Rosa over to a family who wanted a pet—and a hunting dog. They were delighted; I was disappointed, but relieved as well. Since that time, I encountered a very skilled trainer who had self-trained her own pointer to be a service dog. They were a truly impressive team, and my hat is off to her. I'm sure it wasn't the easiest job anyone has ever undertaken. Over the years I've been convinced that at least for most programs, the time/cost effectiveness of training hunting dogs for service work was probably lower than would appeal either to sponsors or to clients.

Terriers

Ah yes, the redheads of the dog world! Terriers are undoubtedly some of the smartest dogs. Undoubtedly some of the least affected by situational shyness or nervousness in public. Also some of the least prone to many of the canine genetic diseases. Many small terriers or crosses thereof excel in hearing dog work. But for the purposes of larger dogs working in public settings, the terrier group does not have a lot of excellent candidates, except possibly for use by the most experienced of trainers and clients.

Terriers' sheer force of will and independence, their tendency of aggression to other dogs, and their high percentage of dominant behavior combine, I believe, to make them a poor choice for most assistance dog situations. Conversely, some of the best successes I've had with resident therapy dogs have been with terriers. In resident therapy work, independent canine nature usually works for you rather than against. The last thing you want from a resident therapy dog is for him to bond closely to one person or to a small group. I've seen some (carefully chosen) terriers who think they've died and gone to heaven when they land in a 100-bed facility where almost everyone is competing with treats and petting for their attention. They waltz from room to room, ward to ward, and scarcely ever overlook any opportunity to be admired. The instant someone stops the petting, the terrier is off to find greener pastures.

In the unvarying routine of service dog work, ask a terrier to retrieve something 40 times a day and he's likely to stop and demand an annotated, outlined explanation or else fire up a cigarette and say, "Look chum, whose mouth are we talking about here, anyway? Isn't there something more fun to do?" Terriers are funny, adorable, and highly loyal in their own way. But don't mistake them for the most cooperative of breeds.

Fighting Dogs

Like it or not, there are plenty of dog breeds in our modern society whose origins were in the sport of fighting, whether fighting dog against dog, dog against bear, dog against bull, or whatever the case might have been. To the horror and sadness of today's responsible dog owners, the "sport" of dog fighting is making a strong comeback in underground circles of gambling and various criminal scenes. Such history makes for a rather touchy topic with many fans of the breeds. Under proper management and humane treatment, most such dogs are not inclined at all to be aggressive to people. Their inclination to fight other animals, however, is as deeply ingrained in them as is the Border Collie's to herd livestock.

I cannot go so far as to say that someone could not make a successful service dog from one. But I will say I believe it is inappropriate in most situations because of the risks entailed. The inclinations you are dealing with are not the same as those from guarding breeds, which, by the very nature of the job calls for biddability and reasonable discretion. Not so with the fighters: far too many fighting breeds have been developed for one characteristic that overrides all others, and that is the desire to engage and destroy other animals. With the correct owner, these dogs can be managed very successfully in an appropriate home or working situation. Personally, I do not happen to believe service dog work is one of the appropriate places. For a balanced outlook on these breeds, I would recommend the book Gladiator Dogs.[2]

---

[2] Semencic, Carl, *Gladiator Dogs*. Neptune, NJ: TFH Publications, 1998. This book is out of print, but you may be able to find a used one online at *www.abebooks.com*.

Toys

For individuals whose needed help can be performed by a small dog, the advantages of the toy breeds are many, most already discussed in the earlier section on size. Their general personality presents another benefit. Most toy breeds were developed with a single role in mind: companionship. The majority of them can get enough exercise in the tiniest of apartments, and are otherwise perfectly content to sit beside their owner and keep the sofa warm until their services are needed. Keep in mind, however, that many toys are tough, dominant little beasts, and do merit every bit as careful training as larger dogs. That is a training discussion, certainly, but it bears mentioning to resist the impulse to treat these little canines like human babies. They are not! Beyond that, if you don't need a dog to pull your wheelchair or provide walking support, you might be surprised how many of the common service dog tasks a toy can perform—at a fraction of the upkeep costs.

Mixed Breeds

Crossbreeds have a value of their own, part of which comes from their larger gene pool. Mixed breeds tend to have fewer genetically-inherited medical problems such as allergies, cardiomyopathy, or retinal dysfunctions. Many mixed breed dogs are giving excellent performance as service dogs. The majority of hearing assistance dogs trained by larger programs are small mixed breeds. In some cases, some of the canine family background is evident. In some cases, it's a secret that only God knows and he's not telling.

Among the Mystery Mixes, unless you have extensive experience, choosing one for your service dog is a matter to be approached with the help of a trainer skilled in reading behavioral inclinations. A dog might have three, five, or twenty- eight (or more) breeds in his background. The job will be to determine how his personality is inclined and whether or not that is going to match your situation.

FINAL CONSIDERATIONS

All this chapter has done is to scrape the top-level issues related to breed selection. Again I stress that in-depth research on any prospective breed is a good plan. Concerns about temperament are huge, and should be your primary screening criterion regardless of breed.

Genetic testing also needs proper attention. I believe any breeder ought to be able to show you, at a bare minimum, the results of the following tests:

- **hip and elbow x-rays**, with results verified through an independent agency, such as the Orthopedic Foundation for Animals and/or the University of Pennsylvania's Hip Improvement Program. If such independent analysis has not been done, you should ask for your own vet to be able to review the x-ray film.

- **a normal thyroid test**, ideally you want what is called a "full panel," rather than simply a "T-4 screen."

- **eyes free of disease**, as verified by a Canine Eye Registration Foundation (CERF).

Certain breeds have predispositions to other genetic problems, such as hemophilia or heart trouble. Again, this underscores the need for accurate research. Almost any service dog training program spends considerable money screening potential trainees for these problems. If you expect to protect your effort and expense, you'll do the same. Under no circumstances should you consider this chapter to be an exhaustive—nay, not even a complete—discussion on breed characteristics. (Any good breeder who sees it will be happy to assure you that is not the case.) However, if I can convince you to approach the concept of breed selection with a critical eye, consider the origins and purpose of the dog, and to require proof of a dog's ability to perform the job, you'll be well on your way.

SUGGESTED READING

Dalzell, Bonnie and Jay Russel. *Tips on Choosing the Right Dog*. 14 May 2005. <netpet.batw.net/articles/choosing.dog.frame.html>

Davis, Debi. *From Lap to Laundry: Toy Service Dogs*. 1997. 14 May 2005. <www.deltasociety.org/nsdc/tinysd.htm>

Kilcommons, Brian and Sarah Wilson. *Paws to Consider: Choosing the Right Dog for You and Your Family*. New York: Warner Books, 1999.

Lemonick, Michael D. "A Terrible Beauty," *Time*. Vol. 144, No. 24, December 12, 1994. This article is also available online at *www.time.com/time/archive/preview/0,10987,981964,00.html*

Milani, Myrna. *DogSmart: The Ultimate Guide to Finding the Dog You Want and Keeping the Dog You Find*. Lincolnwood, IL: NTC Publishing Group, 1998. *Note:* This book is currently out of print, but copies can usually be located on *www.abebooks.com*.

Shook, Larry. *The Puppy Report: How to Select a Healthy, Happy Dog*. New York: Ballentine Books, 1995.

Walkowicz, Chris. *The Perfect Match: A Dog Buyer's Guide*. Hoboken, NJ: John Wiley & Sons, 1996.

Walkowicz, Chris. *Choosing a Dog for Dummies*. Hoboken, NJ: John Wiley & Sons, 2001.

Chapter 10:

Obtaining Dogs

Where do service dogs come from? You'll find a wide variety of answers to this question. Many trainers use rescues. Many programs have a breeding and foster program of their own. Some programs use the client's own dog. Plenty of trainers choose a specific dog from a private breeder based on the need of a particular client. Is there one best method? No. Each has advantages and drawbacks.

RESCUES

Most people who love dogs are aware of the massive problem of pet overpopulation. Animal control facilities routinely euthanize many thousands of unwanted pets per year. In many places the euthanasia rate is as high as 75% or more of the animals turned in or captured. As many trainers and programs can assure you, quite a few of these dogs can make highly successful service animals.

However, selecting a "rescued" dog for service work can be a tricky business. In some cases you're guessing about age and breed. Temperament doesn't always show very well when you're trying to assess it in the chaotic confines of an animal shelter. The biggest problem is that, most often, you cannot know much about the dog's background. Many things may have happened, which may affect the dog's outlook on training and on people. You might have a dog who has been "on the streets" for long enough to have developed a sense of needing to fight for its food and life against other dogs. Such tendencies may not be immediately evident since the dog is now in a new set of circumstances and may feel overwhelmed or intimidated. Often problems crop up as nasty little surprises a month or two into training.

In my experience, when you choose a likely looking candidate from the shelter, you'll loose a third to half of them in the initial medical screening for problems with heartworm, joints, thyroid, eyes, or other miscellaneous things. Of those that pass the medical check, probably around half of them will prove to be unsuitable for training for one reason or another. Too rambunctious. Too shy. Too energetic. Not energetic enough. Problematic bad habits. What is "wrong" with a dog may not be anything bad at all, but merely something that makes him unsuitable for the particular client you're trying to match. You may find out the dog is younger than you thought and not finished growing—and he's going to end up too big for what your client needs.

An often-problematic question with a failed rescue dog is… what then? Shelters have varying policies about taking dogs back. Some require it. Some don't like it. If you are returning a dog because of a health problem, odds are that he'll be euthanized. That was always an enormously difficult decision for me to make and I would often take the dog from the program and personally try to find him a home where the health problem (if not too great) would not be an issue. This approach is not very practical and can be a rapidly compounding problem. But if you happen to be a total wimp (like me) about returning a dog to a shelter where there isn't much chance he'll get a home, this aspect of the process can make life very hard on the trainers—not to mention expensive.

For a long time Dogs for Disabled used mostly rescues, but until recent years didn't have a good answer for the failed-dog dilemma. Around 1999, a rescue group was founded for Golden Retrievers by people who were members of our local obedience clubs, and most of whom were very familiar with our training director and training methods. A beautiful and complimentary situation developed where we could call up the rescue group and say, "we need X number of candidates." They already had a pretty good idea what we were looking for, and presto, in a couple of days we'd have a bunch of new dogs to work with, already screened for about half the pertinent medical issues. We would complete the remaining medical screening and enter the dogs in training. Those that were satisfactory, we kept. The rest we returned to the rescue group, where they were all the more adoptable to a pet home for having received some amount of training. Our trainers had great confidence that the homes for the "failed" dogs were being properly screened and that their future was far more secure. It was a bonus for all involved. I think it's likely more rescue groups and programs could work out similar complimentary arrangements.

For assistance dog jobs that are pretty straightforward and mostly a matter of command/response training, I am still in favor of using rescues where possible. It's hard to beat the satisfaction of watching a dog, who might otherwise have been destroyed, make a significant difference in the life of a person.

BREEDING PROGRAMS

Unless a trainer is already a private breeder and has a ready supply of dogs, most service dog breeding programs happen in the larger programs. Indeed, as any service dog program begins to grow, one of the logistical problems you'll face is a steady supply of suitable candidates. It's true that many good candidates can be found among rescues. But most of us who have been involved in the search/selection process will assure you there's an infallible Murphy's Law operating: the supply of dogs is not consistent, and you cannot always be sure of getting what you need. When you hit a frustrating dry spell, and you have clients (who are also very frustrated) banging on the door wanting dogs, your thoughts move to starting a breeding program to ensure supply. Enough experiences with having to spend longer *finding* a particular dog than *training* him can make those thoughts grow.

Besides a consistent supply of trainees, the other advantages are many of those already addressed in Chapter 9. High on the list is predictability of what you are getting. Genetic heritage plays a huge role in a dog's character. With a rescued dog, you're guessing at the genetics by observing the behavior. (And you'd better have a pretty skilled set of folks doing the guessing.) With a dog from a good breeding program, you already know a lot before you start. You also know exactly what has happened in the dog's background and how his training has progressed. You can have a much better idea of why various tendencies develop in the dog and what you can expect in the future.

So far as I have been able to determine, the fail-out ratio of dogs from breeding programs is roughly similar to rescued dogs. That is always a matter of concern to those who love dogs and especially those who donate time, money, and effort to help with the general canine overpopulation. The breeding programs do, indeed, create dogs that don't fit the needed profile for service dog work. For the most part, it's not that difficult to place such dogs in regular homes as pets, and many people are delighted to receive a dog that has had such careful rearing and training.

I have heard the adoption segment of breeding programs criticized because the adoptive pet homes could otherwise take other animals from shelters. Certainly, we have far too many extraneous dogs in this country. However, the relative handfuls of "extras" created by responsible programs are a drop in the bucket compared to the many thousands from the puppy mills. Furthermore, any service dog breeding program will constantly be working (on health, temperament, and training) to increase the number of viable candidates, and they do not dump their extra dogs in shelters. A focused breeding effort within an good training program serves a distinct purpose in quantity and quality that could not otherwise be met. The debate ultimately distills to whether the programs choose to meet the needs of the clients—or not. Some larger programs are going to *have* to use breeding to ensure a reliable supply of appropriate dogs. There are far more effective ways to reduce pet overpopulation than to diminish breeding programs that produce desperately needed service animals.

BUYING FROM A BREEDER

For a less experienced trainer, especially one working on his own rather than through a program, I believe buying from a breeder is a highly recommended route. One of the best actions you can take to ensure success is to find a good breeder with an established line of dogs who will help you out in selection—and even with some of the training procedures. By doing so, you greatly increase the amount of practical experience going into your project. Furthermore, with a responsible breeder, you have some options if the dog turns out not to be suitable. Any breeder worth the name would take the dog back and try to match you up with another candidate. Ask such a question before you buy. If the answer is "no," look elsewhere.

Most people who have a well-established line of dogs (of almost any breed) would be thrilled to see one of their dogs working as an assistance dog—so long as the job, the dog, the client, and the situation all match. If the breeder doesn't think so, I strongly advise you listen. Again, keep in mind that it's a feather in the cap for most breeders to have a dog succeed in such a placement. They're unlikely to discourage you for any reason except the obvious—they don't think it's going to work. *Please*, rely on their practical experience! Some of these folks have been evaluating homes and placing dogs of their breed for decades—perhaps since before you knew how to pronounce "dog." Listen and heed. Regardless of your level of training experience, if you need a dog with definite predisposition to certain actions, buying from a reputable breeder is probably the safest route.

PRE-OWNED DOGS

While "pre-owned" sounds like a term from a used car lot, it's all I've ever come up with to correctly describe the process of turning a family or personal pet into a service dog. Dogs for Disabled used to do quite a few of these projects. Then we quit. By no means will I tell you it's not possible. It certainly is possible. And in certain cases very desirable. But the process contains extra challenges that are automatically eliminated by using other routes.

Right from the beginning, anyone considering this route should understand everything that normally applies to the selection process for any service dog applies to your dog, too. Just because he's yours and wonderful and beautiful and smart and loved (yeah, yeah, yeah…I know all that! Mine are too!) does not mean he's appropriate for service dog work. But let's assume he passes all the same tests and meets all the criteria (including rigorous health screening) normally applied to any other candidate. You still face greater challenges than you would starting with a new dog.

Any experienced dog trainer can tell you that dogs are extremely situational in their learning process.[1] This is why a dog will often make a liar out of you when you try to show off his very "well-known" new trick to your friends. The dog isn't deliberately seeking to embarrass you. But he knows the command and the trick in a certain set of circumstances—which includes you and him and possibly some other family members, in a certain setting. When you add guests to the picture, you've changed the circumstances, and the dog may have no clue what's going on. It's a different setting to him. It takes time to get a dog to adequately generalize his training to include the idea that "sit" means sit, whether in the front yard, the back yard, the kitchen, while waiting for dinner, at the park, or at the vet's office. Different dogs require different numbers of variations before they learn the skill of generalization.

This is all pretty basic dog training theory, but it can get amazingly complicated when you attempt to train a pet to be a service dog. Unless your dog has been reared in your home with the correct expectations for future behavior, you have a complex task ahead when you ask him to reorder his life to accommodate a job. This will be particularly true if you send him away to "school." I lost count of how many dogs I saw go through this process, then go back home and show by their actions that they were thinking, "Whew! Am I ever glad *that* is over! I'm home now and things can get back to normal." Whether "normal" meant disruptive behavior, digging in the back yard, 10-hour play times while owner is at work, or simply not having to do much of

---

[1] For an excellent presentation of dogs as situational learners, see Connie Cleveland's article, "How Do Dogs Learn" at *www.dogtrainersworkshop.com*.

anything specific, it's all extra baggage that the owner must work through. Whereas a new trainee has never been in the home in anything other than working conditions. He's less likely to assume he can re-institute old behaviors.

Can this problem be worked around? Sure it can. Especially if your dog is well-suited by temperament to service dog work. Even more so if you, the person needing the service dog, have a good knowledge of your dog and a reasonable amount of training experience. But it probably does mean extra training hours and a less effective time/expense ratio, which is exactly what most service dog programs are supposed to avoid. When you are running a non-profit program that stays alive on donated funds, you are responsible to get the greatest mileage out of every dollar. When you face the choice between "workable" and "quicker and workable for less money," the choice isn't really a choice at all.

To be as fair as I know how, if you are an experienced dog person and have a good candidate already in your home, this approach might be your best route. If you need help trying, there are programs to which you can go that specialize in this sort of training.[2] But be aware you are taking a greater burden of responsibility on yourself—particularly if you choose to self-train with no outside help whatsoever. It's legal. It's possible. But I cannot overstress the importance of doing your homework. Pay careful attention to legal considerations and be sure to provide adequate protection for yourself, for your dog, and for those around you.

---

[2] One such program I am aware of, but not otherwise familiar with, is Pets and People. Their phone number is 251-866-2226.

Chapter 11:

Evaluating Temperament

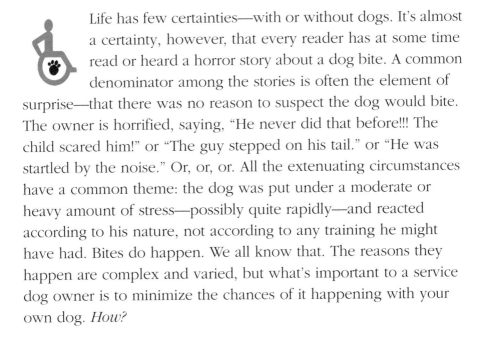
Life has few certainties—with or without dogs. It's almost a certainty, however, that every reader has at some time read or heard a horror story about a dog bite. A common denominator among the stories is often the element of surprise—that there was no reason to suspect the dog would bite. The owner is horrified, saying, "He never did that before!!! The child scared him!" or "The guy stepped on his tail." or "He was startled by the noise." Or, or, or. All the extenuating circumstances have a common theme: the dog was put under a moderate or heavy amount of stress—possibly quite rapidly—and reacted according to his nature, not according to any training he might have had. Bites do happen. We all know that. The reasons they happen are complex and varied, but what's important to a service dog owner is to minimize the chances of it happening with your own dog. *How?*

CRITERIA FOR ANALYSIS
No absolute rule exists to guarantee a dog will never bite. The nature of dogs, illnesses, injuries, and circumstances are too widely

varied, and any dog knows how to bite and is capable of causing serious injury. So this chapter is dedicated to the topic of minimizing—not eliminating—risk. Service dog owners must consider this question from the perspective of *unexpected circumstances,* not according to what is relatively normal in the dog's surroundings. We have already discussed how correct training can mitigate problems and assure your dog's reactions in normal circumstances. For such evaluations, "normal" needs to be thought of as something that happens routinely—if not every day, at least now and then. "Normal" means something that can be anticipated, planned for, and trained for.

While it's important to assess a dog's reaction to many types of normal activity, his reaction to the abnormal—the surprising and potentially disagreeable—needs a good investigation, also. Perhaps especially when thinking of that unexpected something that might happen only once in a dog's career, you would want to know a dog's potential reaction. What if he was badly startled or perhaps given reason to think he was threatened? For instance, let's suppose you're in a store somewhere, passing an elevator door. When the door opens, two young boys burst out, racing toward the exit and their ride home. Maybe they're wearing Halloween costumes and masks. Perhaps they don't even see your dog and trip and fall right over top of him. Candy and bags are flying everywhere; kids are yelling. The dog has a paper bag stuck on his head, and you just dropped the leash. What's going to happen?

UNPLANNED TESTS

In my own training experience, I gained great respect for such questions as a result of two incidents that happened close together very early in my training years. One day I was in a store with a service dog trainee. This particular store was a regular stop, and the owners had been extremely cooperative about allowing trainees to accompany me. Almost every employee knew me and several were interested in the dogs. This particular day, I was standing in the checkout line, one eye on the trainee, Dillon (a very nice Australian Shepherd), and one on the check I was writing. I had absolutely no warning except for perhaps a half second's impression that someone was directly behind me. Before I could even turn my head, a very large young man, clearly an individual with Down Syndrome, had snatched my trainee off the floor and was hugging him as he might have a toy. "Hi, Doggiedoggiedoggie!!!" the young man crooned, with his face pressed against the dog's head and muzzle. To his everlasting and wonderful credit, Dillon hung in the young man's grasp without any dispute beyond a protesting wiggle. The boy's horrified father quickly put an end to the session and apologized profusely. I was a bit too stunned to do more than nod, pat the dog, and note that every employee in sight was staring at the scene with wide eyes and open mouth. They and I all shared an identical thought: what if Dillon had not been so agreeable? The abruptness of the action alone might have drawn a sharp response. I left the store giving much thought to how one might assess a dog's reflexive response to unpredictable and stressful situations.

Less than a week later, I was in a public park with another trainee, a Labrador mix, Lady, introducing her to moving around with a wheelchair. The park was a virtual maze of sidewalks and was at the time one of my favorite places to train. Lady was a rescue, and though she'd been friendly and relaxed enough so far, none of us knew much about her background. Since it was very early in her training, I was concentrating heavily on the dog and missed the development of a nasty prank from a bunch of teenagers until it was already underway. They had decided it would be funny to gang up and "dive-bomb" the dog by whizzing closely by with their bikes and trying to bump her. While their game immediately lost much of its "fun" when they discovered I was neither confined to the chair nor willing to tolerate their nonsense, the reaction from the dog was highly informative. Lady panicked. Her reaction was a blend of spinning, snapping, hackling, urinating, and bucking like a little bronco. Nor could she bring it under control even after the teens had dispersed. There were other bicycles in the park and clearly she now considered them the very instruments of the devil. It took me about 15 minutes of repetitive work and gentle, persistent urging to produce a correct response that I could praise. I was a pretty novice trainer at the time, but I left the park with a single strong impression: I was awfully glad Lady wasn't the one who got grabbed in the store.

When told about the episode, the program training director instantly recognized the symptoms of what most dog trainers call "bad nerve." Lady never went in public again; she was failed out of the training program. Her behavior was a classic example of one kind of dog found in the horror stories we referred to at the beginning of this chapter—an outwardly easy-going dog who becomes a news flash when a child gets mauled. Such a dog finds himself in a situation he perceives as threatening. With no escape available, the dog lashes out in what it considers to be self-defense. A fear-biter. Contrast this behavior with Dillon's, who might very well have believed himself under attack and responded accordingly. He did not. It's important to find out as early as possible which type you're dealing with!

PLANNED TESTS

Most trainers have their favored methods for assessing temperament. You may be the trainer, or the client, or you might be fulfilling both roles. But someone will be responsible for choosing the service dog candidate. Assuming you are considering a particular source, and assuming you are evaluating an adult dog, ask the current owner all the questions you can think of about how they assess temperament. Be specific. Record or write down the information you're given. Ask for demonstrations. If you are comfortable with what you see, and the dog looks relaxed, happy, and friendly... move to phase two, implementing planned tests.

Startle Responses and Recovery

Think up something startling or strange that might happen where you live or work. Ask to see the dog put in such circumstances and watch his reaction. Ideally you'd like to see this test happen with the dog's current owner, but if that's not possible, have a third party handle him so that you can watch. Think about loud, noisy, and abrupt: garbage trucks banging dumpsters around, aircraft traffic, construction sites, a passer-by who rattles and drops a noisy shopping bag near (or on) the dog, a pyramid of empty soda cans knocked over as the dog is passing, or anything else safe and creative you can think of. Perhaps even an "accidental" step on his toe or tail. (Gently, please! Just enough to pinch a bit.) Such an accident is nearly guaranteed to happen during a service dog's working life—and not necessarily gently.

Whatever the circumstance created, please understand that it's okay for a dog to be startled! Enough of a racket or a surprise will startle anyone—canine or human. In fact if the circumstances you're using to test the dog don't cause a startle response, it won't be much of a test. What you are looking for is what happens in those few seconds following the startle response, and how long the dog takes to recover. Plan ahead, and be ready to watch the dog carefully immediately after he is startled. A videotape of the test would be especially helpful, since you could review it several times to be sure of what you are seeing. Better yet, you can show it to someone else for a second opinion. A few specific questions to consider are listed below:

- Y/N   Will the dog willingly re-approach the area where he was startled or does he hang back and look afraid?
- Y/N   Does the dog hackle? Raising the hair along the spine is a sure sign of excitement—and most often nervousness and uncertainty. A brief fur ruffling might be okay if it disappears quickly. But if the hackling is pronounced, or if it stays…be very careful of this dog!
- Y/N   Does the dog crouch and/or lean backwards? These also are signs of worry or concern.
- Y/N   If a reluctant dog is urged to move forward, does he show any aggression toward the handler?
- Y/N   If he has to be forced to move forward, does the dog respond with growling?
- Y/N   Does the dog cower and/or urinate?
- Y/N   Does the dog show aggressiveness or inclination to charge forward and attack? If the dog's tail, head, and ears are all extremely erect, his body posture is leaning forward, and he is holding direct eye contact with any person or animal, then he is at least thinking about being aggressive, even if he's not actually growling or charging.

Any "Yes" answers should be considered negatively, although the degree of response should be factored in. That is, a mild unwillingness to re-approach, or a slight ducking of the head and posture might be one thing. Or a raised tail by itself would probably be okay, so long as the dog is not giving off a whole set of "challenge signals." However, if you truly want the best prospect for a service dog, you will eliminate any candidate that shows any of these responses in a pronounced way. Could such a dog be adequately socialized or desensitized to live safely and happily as a companion? Yes, most of them, probably. But that's not what you are looking for. You want to start with the *best* prospect possible, not what can be manipulated to work most of the time. Resist any urge to feel sorry for a disqualified dog because he's frightened, or because he might not get another chance. That may or may not be true. But he's all wrong and definitely unsafe for a service dog.

You should keep in mind one other important factor: a dog does not have to be completely non-reactive during a test. There is a difference between exhibiting fear and showing curiosity. If a dog wants to approach with neutral curiosity (wagging tail, relaxed posture) and examine the new object, or investigate the source of the noise, that's good, not bad! Training will, in time, explain to him what is to be focused on or ignored. It's common for a good dog who is confronted by a new, loud, and/or strange stimulus to want to know exactly what the new thing is, and how it smells, looks, acts, and responds. I'm not referring to an aggression; that's not what you're looking for. But a response of pronounced curiosity should not be faulted. A dog who wants to investigate is showing predisposition to get more information, not make a snap judgment. That's a highly desirable trait.

Working in New Circumstances

Beyond the implementation of a "startle test," there are other procedures that can tell you something about a dog's level of confidence and stability. Ideally, you should see a dog work in a variety of circumstances, not just one or two. Consider the following suggestions, and put together a list of how many you could expose a dog to in whatever available time you have. Plan for as many as you can—don't just go out hoping to find something. The more circumstances in which you see a dog worked, the more you'll be able to see his potential for reliability and/or unstable reactions. Here are some examples:

Surroundings	schools, grocery stores, parks, malls, private homes, offices
Acoustics	quiet office versus the hollow hubbub of a large building or stadium
Footing	carpet, slick floors, sidewalk gratings, walkover bridges
Traffic	heavy street traffic, large trucks, bicycles
Animals	other dogs, cats, livestock, birds, squirrels, rabbits
Children	playground, busy neighborhood, tricycles, noisy toys
Transportation	in and out of cars, buses, taxis, or trains
Misc/weird	a reflecting wall surface, a glass-sided elevator, a moving sidewalk
Noise	aircraft takeoff/landing, trains, factories, thunderstorms, guns, fireworks, popping/crackling fire in a fireplace

Any substantial, obvious worry or hesitation from a dog to any of the above (or to any similar conditions) should raise a large red flag to you. Any excuses that "well, the dog has never seen this before…give him a chance to get used to it" should not alter your judgement. *Lack of exposure does not matter.* In fact, lack of exposure is precisely what you're looking for! The dog's initial response to something new and potentially stressful is exactly what you want to see. For the dog to slow down slightly, look carefully, or show distractible curiosity is all fine. Those are training issues. Any refusal to work, crouching, trembling, growling, or other symptoms as described earlier should eliminate this dog from your consideration. Those are temperament problems.

If at all possible, when considering a dog's reliability in varied circumstances, avoid making a decision about any candidate on the basis of a single session. For one thing, you cannot possibly expose the dog to enough new situations in any single session. For another, if a new trainer is the one handling the dog, rather than the dog's owner, the dog might act differently than he would with his owner with whom he is completely comfortable. Another trainer's newness might be nothing beyond simple curiosity on the dog's part. He's intrigued by the new person and less tuned in to what else is nearby. It might take some time for him to get to know the trainer and return to his average/normal response—which might be either better or worse than what's seen at first.

Ideally, even if you choose to try a dog in training, you want to have the option of returning him within a few weeks if he proves unsuitable. During the interim you should repeatedly expose him to as many new, strange, and varied scenarios as possible. Especially if you were not able to observe the dog working with his "own person," you might be surprised how differently a dog acts after he gets to know you. Better, you think, because he gets more used to things? Not necessarily! In the beginning, he might be paying more attention to a new trainer, just *because* the trainer is new—and therefore interesting—than to something else nearby. As the trainer becomes less novel and more of a known quantity, you might see the dog become much more worried about or reactive to the environment around him. Yesterday he might not have even seen some weird-looking object on the path; today, as he's less intrigued with the trainer and now looking around, he thinks, "Yikes! What is that??"

Composite Pictures

Usually after the first week or so of training—often far less time—a good trainer can predict fairly accurately how a dog will respond to either a startle test or to most new circumstances. Each response a dog gives to almost anything, even in normal surroundings, provides a piece of information about temperament. How a dog responds to a correction or inducement to a new behavior is part of the evaluation process. If he falls to emotional pieces at the first adversity or difficult task, that tells you something. If he tries to bite you, that tells you something else. Any trainer will be interested in whether a dog is fearful of new elements, extremely friendly to strangers, or territorial about people approaching his vehicle. The accumulation of single responses grows into a valuable picture.

However, I would still advise you to pursue formal testing. No matter how perfectly your service dog is trained, you still face the possible wildcard of some frightening or highly pressured event somewhere in your dog's career. In a moment of abrupt and strong stress, a dog will react according to his nature, not his training. And the reaction might happen in a fraction of a second before you could possibly have a chance to give a command or eliminate the problem. In addition, over time, a series of similar, repetitive stressors might eventually cause a dog to develop a strengthening, negative response. Thus, considering a dog's natural temperament is just as important as considering his training—possibly more so. You would not want to waste time or money training a dog whose temperament was not satisfactory for the job. No absolute guarantee exists, but I believe it's advisable to do everything possible to reduce risk.

GENETIC PREDISPOSITION

Whether you are a client, a trainer, a sponsor, or a parent, the most critical point to understand about canine temperament is this. A dog's routine behavior might change to some degree with training; however, *the essential composition of a dog's temperament does NOT change with training.* A dog is what he is. Canines do not rationalize and analyze their actions in the same way humans do. Consequently, when inserted into situations they perceive as seriously dangerous, dogs *will* default to self-preservation behaviors. The operative question, then, is how difficult (or easy) is it to make the dog think he is in danger? His basic level of confidence, not training, determines that answer. That degree of confidence is what the term "soundness" describes.

Bookstores, trainers, veterinarians, and behaviorists are all full of information and suggestions about socializing and acclimating worried, overly sensitive, or overly aggressive dogs from infancy through adulthood. All such information is helpful, and necessary for many owners, for many reasons. But service dogs should be measured with a different yardstick. The question is not "how completely can the dog be fixed," but "how sound is the dog in the beginning?" Socialization and training can address only sufficient exposure and conditioning to decrease the circumstances in which the dog perceives threat. But in new circumstances, that basic nature is still there!

It's worthwhile to note that every dog on the planet has a mental and/or emotional melting point. Any dog could somehow, someway eventually be pressed into self-defense mode. This is why a badly-injured dog—even your own well-trusted buddy—is likely to bite you when you try to help him. He's not being nasty on purpose: he's being a dog. On far milder levels, a dog who reflexively lashes out at something new and startling is exhibiting pretty much the same self-defense behavior. The difference is in the amount of stimulation needed to produce the reaction.

To incorporate a dog with weak temperament into a family or a known circumstance is far easier than putting a working dog on the street. Many variables can be controlled. Most people in contact with the dog know the situation. Everybody can learn together and the result can be intensely rewarding for all humans and canines. It is not, in any way, my intent to belittle that. Dogs are not perfect any more than people are, and dogs don't have to be perfect to be loved and appreciated. Some of my best obedience competition dogs have been those who had profound weaknesses of temperament. In fact, one in particular was actually pretty crazy. And I loved her anyway, craziness and all. But despite the large pile of blue ribbons and awards, I would never, *never* have taken her out as a service dog! Many very impressive competition dogs have serious temperament flaws. It doesn't mean they're not good at what they do—but it wouldn't make them good service dogs. Such distinctions lead directly back to the difference between the quality of the training and the quality of the dog, as addressed in Chapter 5.

Because of the element of unpredictable circumstances and sudden surprises (which will never be completely—or even substantially—under the control of the handler), safe service dog training demands the choice of a dog whose temperament is as completely sound and non-reactive as possible. As previously said about corrections, if you use a training method that's totally free of corrections, you cannot know how good your training is until your dog gets a better offer than whatever reward you're controlling. The guiding principle with canine temperament is similar: *you cannot know how a dog will respond to stress if he is never exposed to it.* Corollary: I believe that to fail to allow the dog to undergo stress in a measured, deliberate manner during training (for the purpose of evaluation) is to gamble on the dog's later response to unpredictable stress in public. Might a handler/owner merely take pains to avoid such problems? Maybe. Nothing might ever happen. But with dogs I own or train, I consider that a heck of a gamble with fate. You could have a great working relationship for half a dozen years…then one day an oblivious pedestrian accidentally steps on your dog's tail and Rover loses his mind to aggressive panic. It only takes one time for somebody to get hurt. I prefer getting some clues ahead of time and weeding out candidates with unacceptable responses.

The ideal service dog candidate stays relaxed and interested in his surroundings regardless of who is holding the leash. He is either oblivious to or curious about new things, not anxious about noise or changes of footing, recovers quickly and remains steady when startled, and shows no aversion to approaching strangers or passing near them. If those things are not true about a dog you're considering, do everybody—including the dog—a favor and rule him out. He would be no more happy in a life as a service dog than you would be having him as such.

TESTS IN THE PAST

During the years in which most dog breeds were developed, dogs had a far more utilitarian status than do most of today's pampered family members (my own included, I should add). If you are considering the selection, support, or training of a dog for service work, you'd do well to keep in mind that many, if not most, of the dogs coming out of show-winning kennels are *not* selectively bred according to a performance standard, but only according to a show standard. In most cases, if the dog looks the best (according to the current market trends), behaves best in the ring, does not eat the judge, and moves the most correctly (also according to current market trends), then it's considered a good and valuable dog. This practice certainly has absolutely nothing to do with the dog's working or performance ability.

In the past, most dogs had a purpose. If they were incapable of serving said purpose safely and reliably, without extra effort, time, expense, or coddling, out they went—out of the gene pool, and often out of life itself. While such an unrelenting standard can make many of us modern pet lovers wince, it was exactly this stringency of evaluation that created the useful breeds we know and love today. Unfortunately, the vast overpopulation of dogs is much aided and abetted by casual, indiscriminate breeding practices from those who do not use a tough performance standard for choices in canine reproduction.

While I am no advocate of euthanasia for every dog of questionable temperament (and it should go almost without saying that they don't belong in jobs as service animals), I am definitely an advocate of sterilization for every dog of questionable temperament. I find the perpetuation of non-functional, dangerous traits in dogs to be a shameful failing on the part of breeders throughout the country. Even the majority of conformation show champions do not have a single temperament qualification required to obtain their status. While this is most definitely a matter of personal choice, not legality, the broad range of resulting temperament problems calls for hyper-vigilance on the part of a buyer. Both the trainer and the client inherit an enormous burden of proof for ensuring general humanity's safety around your service dog. If you don't voluntarily take up the burden and make sure of what you are getting into, you may find yourself facing the same burden of proof in court—after some full-fledged disaster with the dog. Be critical. Be picky. Be safe. Be sure.

> **Note** If you are interested in a more in-depth examination of temperament issues, and especially if you plan to use a breed with protective tendencies as a service dog, read Appendix A.

Chapter 12:

Legal Considerations

Please note that the title to this chapter is *not* "Legal Advice." In no way should any comments here be construed to replace counsel from a licensed attorney. As with all substantive questions in this book, individual situations are far too varied for any list of rules to apply successfully to all of them. As always, my intent is to give a reasonable framework on which you can do your own research. That intent is even stronger with this material, which is, by necessity, essentially an extended list of questions—*not* answers! The questions might, in fact, make an good basis of discussion between you and your own lawyer.

No topic in today's society can be considered properly without sufficient attention to legal context. It's hard to pick up a newspaper anymore without hearing about a new ordinance, lawsuit, or piece of pending legislation about dogs. How those things interact with your specific ownership and use of a service dog is something I highly recommend you work through before you admit a service animal to your home, far more so before you take any such dog into a public setting.

Beyond issues of liability, individuals spending large amounts of money and/or time on the acquisition of a service dog likely want some legal commitment from the seller or the trainer that the dog will perform according to reasonable expectations. You also have the issues to face of how your right to use a service dog in public might conflict with the equally important rights of other people.

LIABILITY

We have already discussed at some length the range of bizarre scenarios one can face in public with a dog. The logical extension is to document your protection if something untoward should happen during the years of the dog's working life. If you are obtaining a dog through an established training program, the first thing to establish is whether or not there is any shared liability for the dog's conduct. In most cases, the answer to this will be "no," but it is worth checking. Most training organizations are certainly willing to back you up on the quality of the dog's selection and training, but it is almost impossible for any trainer to guarantee what happens outside of his sight or control. If the dog's owner does not adhere to instruction, almost anything can happen. Therefore it's unlikely that a trainer will voluntarily assume liability for a dog's public behavior. What part, if any, of finally-sustained claims the trainer might be liable for is a matter you will want to address in a contract. We'll get to that later.

INSURANCE

Many homeowner's, or even renter's, insurance policies provide liability protection for pets, but keep in mind that a service dog is not a pet. Whatever your existing coverage for personal property and liability, you'll want to call your agent to determine what kind of coverage you would or would not have regarding your service dog. In most cases, my recommendation to service dog users is to obtain a "personal umbrella" policy that provides additional liability protection. Such coverage typically costs $15-20 extra per month on any existing policy. The odds that you will actually ever need it are small. But that's why we call it "insurance." Believe me, if you ever need it, you may really, *really* need it. Above all, if your intent is to rely on an existing policy for coverage, *call your agent.* This is no place for guesswork or surprises.

Also to be considered under personal property insurance is the matter of whether or not the cost of replacing your dog would be covered if an accident took his life. While it is not pleasant to consider such things, $10,000 or more is hard enough to come by the first time around. If your dog were killed in a home fire, for instance, or a traffic accident, would your personal insurance policy cover his replacement? Find out!

Finally, you may want to give consideration to pet health insurance. This is a much newer field, and so far as I can evaluate, not terribly effective just yet for routine matters. But it may be worth exploring what it would cost to cover life-threatening and expensive conditions such as bloat or traumatic injury in a car accident.

ACCESS

One of the best references about access is from the US Department of Justice, in their publication titled *Frequently Asked Questions about Service Animals in Places of Business*.[1] In short, anyone using a service dog has the right to take that dog almost anywhere in public places. However, that "almost" in the previous sentence still has validity. The right of accommodation is not absolute. The

---

[1] You can read this United States Department of Justice document online at *www.usdoj.gov/crt/ada/svcanimb.htm*. Or you can call (800) 514-0301 for further information.

CHAPTER 12: LEGAL CONSIDERATIONS

presence of a service dog in any public place cannot present a danger to anyone else present. The dog cannot fundamentally change the nature of the service or location. Nor can the dog's presence or actions prohibit others' normal use and/or enjoyment of the place.

Consider these examples, the first few related to behavior. If your dog can't be still and quiet during a performance, theater management has every right to remove him. If your dog will not stop lifting his leg on (or sampling) the groceries, he's out of the store, and rightfully so. If a dog threatens, attempts, or succeeds in biting someone, any reasonable place will show you the door.

Some restrictions are not related to behavior, but merely to the presence of the dog. If there is an all-feline veterinarian in your town who promotes his clinic on the premise that no client's cat will be stressed by the presence of dogs, then the presence of a service dog (even if the owner is taking a cat for treatment) would fundamentally alter the nature of the service provided. A dog could reasonably be excluded no matter how well-behaved he is. If you are visiting a family member in a hospital's intensive care ward—don't expect to take your dog inside the ward and place patients at additional risk. Dogs cannot sterilize their hands and wear scrubs. If the presence of your service dog at the zoo throws a resident animal into defensive or predatory spasms, the management would be within reason to ask you to move on, otherwise the dog's presence might damage the exhibited animal or cause the animal to pose a threat to visitors or handlers.

As I have told each client over the years: the public gets almost no choice about having your dog among them. Your corresponding duty is to be reasonable. It's not all that difficult to tell if someone is trying to resolve a problem, or if he just doesn't want a dog around. A disabled individual has a right to assistance from a service dog. But that right cannot deprive other people of their rights, either. In other words, if you find yourself in an airplane cabin, with your dog, seated next to someone with a violent allergy to dogs…please do all other service dog owners a favor and don't threaten to sue the airline if they need to move you to a different seat. Your fellow passenger has a right to breathe, also.

On the other hand, if you encounter someone in public who is adamant about "no dogs allowed in here" and will not listen to your explanation that the dog is a service animal, I advocate an absolute no-mercy response. The ADA is now a decade and a half old; to borrow a piece of current slang, it is "way time" that people get clued in. When any individual or administration is unwilling to accommodate service animals simply because they don't think they have to or believe they can successfully bully the owner of the dog, I am strongly in favor of forcing the issue, even to the point of legal action, if necessary.

TRAINEES

A canine trainee who is learning to become a service dog is *not* a service dog. The federal statute that allows service dogs in public places, Public Law 101-336, gives the "right" to the person with the disability, not to the dog. Therefore, unless an individual state has granted additional rights to trainers, a trainee service dog is not allowed in a public place without permission of the owner of the establishment. If you are considering training your own service dog, you would do well to keep this in mind. Until such time as you are prepared to say, "This is my service animal," and to take full responsibility for the results of your statement, you'll need to obtain permission from the owner of any building or location where you want to take a trainee.

BREED-SPECIFIC RESTRICTIONS

A good source of continuing information on nationwide issues about breed-specific issues is available in the "Legislative Alert" section of the American Kennel Club's electronic newsletter, *Taking Command*.[2]

EMPLOYMENT

How does the ADA interact with an individual's employment? Does any employer have to allow an employee to use a service dog on the job? So far as I can determine, this remains a rather gray area. The ADA "requires covered entities, including private employers, to provide reasonable accommodations to the known physical or mental limitations of an otherwise qualified individual with a disability who is an applicant or employee, unless such covered entity can demonstrate that the accommodation would impose an undue hardship."[3] The definition of "undue hardship" is left rather open-ended. However, some of the qualifying situations wouldn't be terribly hard to visualize. A dog can present a substantial threat to others' safety or a fundamental change in the nature of some business settings just by his presence. Consider how the a dog might complicate or jeopardize the business underway in a hospital, a food production area, a variety of industrial/assembly functions, or the sterile conditions of a research lab.

While the above seems fairly clear-cut, matters may not always be as simple as they seem. Complicating the confusion even more are the actual "definitions" of a disability. If you are contemplating a service animal at your job, a good starting point of research might be to read through the Supreme Court Decision,

---

[2] The AKC newsletter is online at *www.akc.org/enewsletter/taking_command*.
[3] 42 U. S. C. §12112(b)(5)(A) (1994 ed.); see also §12111(2) ("The term 'covered entity' means an employer, employment agency, labor organization, or joint labor_management committee.")

CHAPTER 12: LEGAL CONSIDERATIONS

Toyota vs. Williams (No. 00-1089), rendered January 8, 2002.[4] Though the case did not involve service animals, it had a lot to do with the ADA. Ms. Williams challenged Toyota, her employer for a change or adaptation (based on the ADA) in working conditions because of her disability of carpal tunnel syndrome. The Court found for Toyota, despite recognizing that the woman did indeed have carpal tunnel syndrome. Specifically, the court stated that Ms. William's disability, though valid, was not of the nature which the ADA was designed to protect. One section from the majority opinion (by O'Conner for a unanimous court) is particularly interesting to me:

> (a) The Court's consideration of what an individual must prove to demonstrate a substantial limitation in the major life activity of performing manual tasks is guided by the ADA's disability definition. "Substantially" in the phrase "substantially limits" suggests "considerable" or "to a large degree," and thus clearly precludes impairments that interfere in only a minor way with performing manual tasks. Cf. *Albertson's, Inc.* v. Kirkingburg, 527 U.S. 555, 565. Moreover, because "major" means important, "major life activities" refers to those activities that are of central importance to daily life. In order for performing manual tasks to fit into this category, the tasks in question must be central to daily life. To be substantially limited in the specific major life activity of performing manual tasks, therefore, an individual must have an impairment that prevents or severely restricts the individual from doing activities that are of central importance

---

[4] An easy-to-view copy of the majority opinion is online at *http://caselaw.lp.findlaw.com/*. Select the section for Supreme Court decisions, then the year 2002, then find Toyota versus Williams on the alphabetical listing.

to most people's daily lives. The impairment's impact must also be permanent or long-term. See 29 CFR §§§§1630.2(j)(2)(ii-iii).

....

It is insufficient for individuals attempting to prove disability status under this test to merely submit evidence of a medical diagnosis of an impairment. Instead, the ADA requires them to offer evidence that the extent of the limitation caused by their impairment in terms of their own experience is substantial.

While no one in the legal community has thus far asked my opinion, it appears to me there is still some disparity to be found about what actually constitutes a disability meriting ADA protection. Though it does not relate specifically to employment, consider, for example, the policies of the Federal Aviation Administration and the Transportation Security Administration, which arise from §14 CFR Part 382, "Nondiscrimination on the Basis of Disability in Air Travel."[5] The FAA allows a broad range of service animals to travel with their owners, and no distinction of impairment of a major life function is required. In fact, the policy even includes animals that function as "emotional support," though the need for such animals must be documented by a mental health professional.[6]

While it's not my intention to confuse any issues, or to load readers down with legal technicalities, there is a point to all this: don't assume! Recognize that the culture and legal arena in which you function with your service dog is a rather fluid, in-motion place. When new circumstances loom, take responsibility to do

---

[5] You can view this document at *airconsumer.ost.dot.gov/rules/382SHORT.htm*.
[6] Excellent information, as well as excellent perspective in viewing matters from the point of view of the airlines, is available at *airconsumer.ost.dot.gov/rules/guidance.htm*. Choose the document titled, "Service Animal Guidance."

some research. Since you are the one initiating the service dog/owner relationship, you are assuming a responsibility for a "continuing education" of sorts. New legislation tomorrow or next month could alter the picture significantly.

As a help toward this process, I would encourage you to read through at least some of the articles on the web site of the International Association of Assistance Dog Partners (IAADP) at *www.iaadp.org*. IAADP is an organization for the users of assistance dogs, not for trainers or programs. You may or may not agree with every position you read at the site, but IAADP does a commendable job of staying up to date with various service dog issues. Many facts are available, along with various opinions, to help you make your own informed decisions.

CONTRACTS

This book doesn't contain many absolutes, but here is one of the few: if you're about to obtain a service dog from any source, you need a contract. No exceptions. Whether your trust your own judgement or require an attorney's input is for you to decide. But the potential for confusion, misunderstandings, inappropriate attention to detail, or lack of follow-through, is far too great *on both sides* to trust a verbal understanding alone. If a service dog placement is going to work, both the owner and the trainer will have to make a substantial commitment, not just for the initial weeks, but for the lifetime of the dog.

Your own circumstances might require additional or more extensive items to be covered. But as a starting point, any contract between a service dog owner and a trainer should clearly and fully answer the following questions:

- Who is responsible to select the dog, and who holds the final right of decision if there is any disagreement on the matter?

- What elements will be performed in the way of medical screening for the dog? Where will this happen? Who is responsible for the costs?
- What tests will be performed in the way of temperament testing for the dog? Where will this take place? Who is responsible for the costs?
- What tests will be performed to ensure successful completion of a dog's training? Where will each take place? Who is responsible for the costs?
- Where will each phase of the training take place? Are there time limits on each phase, and if so, what are they?
- Who is responsible for the dog's care and expenses during training?
- If the dog becomes ill or injured during training, who is responsible for medical costs and how will the illness affect the projected timetable for training?
- Does the trainer have the right to fail a dog during training? If so, whose responsibility is it to replace the dog and complete the previous steps with a new candidate?
- What equipment will the dog require for performing his job? Who is responsible to purchase the equipment? Who is responsible to replace equipment broken during training? Who is responsible to replace equipment as it wears out during normal use?
- At what point does actual ownership of the dog transfer to the client?
- If actual ownership of the dog is retained by the trainer, will he be responsible for veterinary costs during the dog's working life? Who is responsible to transport the dog for

medical care? Who is responsible to provide rehabilitative care for an injury or extended illness?

- What rights, if any, does a trainer have to repossess a dog for a client's failure to pay?

- What rights, if any, does a trainer have to repossess a dog for failure to comply with correct training procedure?

- Who must pay for any travel expenses related to training? And with what frequency?

- How long will the client-training phase last and where will it take place?

- Does the trainer require a certification policy? If so, does it require periodic renewal? At what intervals?

- Does the trainer have the right to replace the dog at his discretion if the dog is not performing acceptably or if the terms of the contract are not met?

- Is there any shared liability for the dog's actions in public after placement? If so, under what conditions? Who is responsible for associated legal costs? Who is responsible for what percentage of any finally-sustained claims?

- Is there a minimum expected working life for the dog? If so, what is it?

- If the dog develops a terminal illness during training or during his working life, whose responsibility is it, and at which stage, to replace the dog?

- If the trainer is unable to continue the terms of the contract due to disability or death, do the terms of the contract transfer to another party? If so to whom?

- If the client is unable to continue using the dog according to the terms of the contract due to life-changing circumstances or death, does the trainer have the right to repossess the dog?
- Under what conditions does either side have the right to terminate the agreement? What kind of notice must be given? If this happens, which party owns the dog?
- A legal jurisdiction should be acknowledged for the purpose of resolving disputes.

SUGGESTED READING

Carroom, Ilene. *Getting Through the Maze.* 1994. 19 May 2005 <www.iaadp.org/maze.html>

Duncan, SL and the 1997, 1998, and 1999 APIC Guidelines Committees. *APIC State-of-the-Art Report: The implications of service animals in health care settings.* 2000 19 May 2005 <www.deltasociety.org/nsdc/dsb720.htm#apic>

Legal Rights Handbook, 8th ed. Santa Rosa, CA: Assistance Dogs International, 2005. To order a copy, see *www.adionline.org/LegalRightsHandbook/law-book.html.*

Randolph, Barbara K. and Mary Randolph. *Dog Law.* Berkeley, CA: Nolo Press, 2002.

Chapter 13:

Resident Therapy Dogs

The concept of using dogs as working residents in hospitals, rehabilitation centers, and long-term care units is not new. Using dogs for visiting, socializing, and relationship building has become extremely popular. Therapy Dogs International[1] certifies privately-owned dogs all across the country to perform regular onsite visits to the sick, disabled, elderly, and young. The benefits are nearly incalculable. Successful arrangements with such dogs predate ADA legislation by many years, and in recent years, more and more facilities are becoming attracted to the concept. Though such dogs are not service animals, per se, and are not included in the federal guidelines, the two have enough parallels and associations (both correct and incorrect) to merit a discussion here.

Other organizations often refer to these canine workers as "Social dogs," "Resident dogs," or "Facility dogs." Differences in terminology are unimportant, except so far as we all know what

---

[1] Therapy Dogs International, 88 Bartley Road, Flanders, NJ 07836. Phone: 973-252-9800.

we're discussing. Dogs For Disabled refers to them as "Resident Therapy Dogs," which is the term I will use.

Most residential facilities are not prepared, or even practically capable, of effectively implementing a resident therapy dog. Personally, I would like to see it happen far more often than it does. Very little can compare with watching a successful dog reduce emotional stress, provide enjoyment and interaction, or elicit responses from folks who won't so much as meet the eyes of the medical staff. However, the practical limitations are immense and definite. Questions of selection, training, legal risk, oversight, and expenses must all be addressed if the organization is not headed down a short route to disaster.

Now that the discouraging news is out of the way, can the concept be made to work? Yes! It can. If the staff begins with a realistic picture, stays in agreement with one another, and sticks to the job, the benefits are too many to catalog here. Anyone who's ever done canine therapy work can tell you story after story about the benefits of a good dog in this job. Sometimes residents who have been in a facility for weeks without saying a single word to anyone—are immediately responsive to a dog. In physical rehabilitation units, I've seen patients who refused even to try their assignments until interaction with a dog became part of the equation. Seemingly endless repetitive arm motions are one thing alone, but perhaps another entirely when the motion is about brushing the therapy dog. In retirement home residents often develop fierce loyalty and camaraderie for "their" dog until the daily care and grooming of the lucky animal becomes an actual raffle item.

Research is replete with findings about mental and physical benefits of pets to humans. All a good therapy dog has to do to be effective is to be a well-behaved pet to the facility—in a manner that does not compromise safety for anyone, including the dog.

The process has many parallels to accommodating any dog in any home—it's just a broader, larger, and far more complicated procedure because of the number of people and the size of the "home."

SELECTION

Though I have not been involved in nearly as many resident therapy dogs placements as service dog placements, there have been enough to develop at least basic guidelines. We used to think (as quite a few folks do) that the correct option was to choose a very friendly, if rather lazy, service dog who was failing out of the training program. We were very wrong! A few remarkably unsuccessful experiences convinced me that the correct profile for a resident therapy dog is quite different from that of a service dog.

Possibly the worst and the best outcomes I've ever observed both happened at the same facility. I share the story here with the permission of the Oakmont Nursing Home of Greenville, South Carolina. Shortly after their decision to obtain a resident therapy dog, they went to the local animal shelter and adopted a likely-looking, perfectly friendly dog, "Lucy." Lucy appeared to be a herding breed mix, perhaps some combination of Border Collie, Australian Shepherd, and who knows what else. Lucy arrived at the facility in a limousine with bows tied around her neck, courtesy of a friend who loved the idea being put into practice. The residents fell in love with the dog. Unfortunately, a mere few days later, Lucy was hiding permanently under the recreation room table, refusing to come out, and threatening anyone who approached her. The staff made the decision to call Dogs for Disabled for help.

Oakmont's intentions were superb, and their commitment to the project remains the highest I've ever encountered. However, their first attempt was a classic case where everything started wrong and went downhill after that. Lucy was a dog with a nervous temperament. She was extremely visual, and, as with many of her breed, had a normal tendency toward a natural protectiveness and territoriality. She had no training and no basis of communication to know what was expected of her. The array of stimuli at her new home was overwhelming to her. Her response was to rely on behaviors natural and comfortable for her: create a "safe zone," guard it, and interact only with one person she happened to trust. I offer this scenario as an example to support my believe that about 90% of having an effective resident therapy dog is a matter of choosing the right dog.

Ultimately, the dog who successfully filled the role of resident therapy dog for Oakmont, was a mixed breed of terrier origins. "Taffy" is not a 24-hour resident, but lives with and attends work with Oakmont's activities director. She is sweet, friendly, and independent enough to have a canine blast cruising room to room to see who has the best petting technique on a given day. Taffy's training was specific to her placement, of course, including such concepts as a fast and fool-proof down, whether to a verbal command or to a tug on her leash—helpful in any case where she might be about to get underfoot, in the way of a potential medical code, or merely in too close contact with someone who might be afraid of dogs, such as a resident's visiting grandchild.

Taffy's introduction to the facility was gradual, making sure at all times she understood how her training applied to each new situation. I've heard that Wall Street traders like the phrase, "the trend is my friend." Well, when it comes to this type of training, the trend will definitely rule—whether as friend or foe. A hugely significant portion of training is to predispose the dog to the habitual behavior you want: make it happen and make it routine. The undesirable behaviors should be altogether prevented from occurring.

When Taffy was not under direct supervision, she was always crated. Eventually she reached the point where such restriction was not necessary. Now, even though she spends the majority of her days with her "boss," the activities director, she is happy and confident in her interaction with the residents. It's a no-contest that she's easily their most popular and sought-after resident.

CAREFUL INTRODUCTION

For a facility considering incorporating such a dog into their environment, they must be prepared for a very rigid initial structure to ensure the dog develops correct habits. How much freedom the dog can have (and when) will depend on the specifics of the situation. In no case, however, is it permissible to allow the dog "free run" of a facility until he has proven by his behavior, under trainer supervision, that he knows what is required and is not only predisposed to do it, but responds well to off-leash direction when corrected. Extremely thorough attention must be given not only to the safety of residents, but also of the dog. In some cases, it's advisable to include a sensor on the dog's collar that activates an alarm if the dog accidentally escapes.

When anyone has approached our program wanting a resident therapy dog, we have many questions and also many requirements before we will agree to participate in the project. In most cases, little is required of the dog beyond friendliness, good manners, and the desire to interact with multiple people. That makes it seem as though surely it couldn't be all that hard…could it? Yes! Much more is required of the staff than of the dog.

HANDLERS

One of the first choices a facility makes is whether or not to have a single person in charge of the dog, as in the scenario with Taffy. In most cases, this is the recommended approach. Though the time the dog spends at work may be more limited, the consistency of handling will likely result in the dog being far more successful in the long-term goal.

If the dog truly will be a 24/7 resident, he will have the proverbial "many masters." No one person works 24/7. Gaining real consistency from multiple handlers is a tall order, and the dog's behavior is virtually guaranteed to be only as good as the worst handler allows. For instance, many medical facilities are staffed on weekends by nursing-provider agencies rather than by direct employees. This can present an enormous challenge for requiring cooperation from all staff. Possible? Yes. Complicated? Yes. It means that the agency who provides your weekend staff has to be in synch with the project every bit as much as the facility's own administration.

PROTECTION

No, not protection *by* the dog. Protection *of* the dog. A resident therapy dog is extremely vulnerable to provocation, or even abuse, at the hands of staff members or visitors who don't like him. A keen eye needs to be kept out at all times, by every staff member. Everyone needs to have clear understanding of what is acceptable behavior *from* the dog and *to* the dog. Any variations or failure to follow procedure are going to result in confusion on the dog's part, and very likely in deteriorating performance.

Another need for constant supervision is merely the liability. You may be familiar with the concept of "professional fallers," a bizarre term I recently heard applied to a woman who had lawsuits pending against 16 stores for negligence because she allegedly fell and injured herself on slick floors. Unbelievable? Don't count on it. If you have a dog loose in a facility where there are regular guests, your staff had better monitor closely. Out-of-sight interaction with non-staff is not a good plan for anyone. If someone should present a false claim that the dog frightened, threatened, or bit them, how do you plan to prove it untrue?

SPECIFIC CONSIDERATIONS

The questions listed below are typical of those we ask any facility before we agree to train or place a dog for them. If you are interested in the possibility, take the time to answer the questions below. While a resident dog can provide enormous benefits for your residents, the scope of the project is large. It will affect almost every aspect of what you do at your facility, consuming significant time and effort from your staff. Unless you already employ a professional trainer, I would strongly recommend you not attempt the project on your own. If in any doubt about that advice, get an opinion from your insurance agent.

In any case, providing detailed answers to the following questions should help you decide if you are ready to undertake the project or not. If you get all the answers sorted out, and still wish to proceed, here's a suggested method of screening your prospective trainers: don't tell them about the list—at least not at first—and see how many of the same questions they ask you on their own. If they don't at least hit the highlights, you're probably not dealing with a someone who has adequate experience for the job.

- Who initiated the idea of a therapy dog in your facility?

- Is there a 100% consensus among your administration on the viability of a resident therapy dog at this facility?

If the answer to the above question is "no," please generally describe the nature of the reservation(s). This will help us to anticipate problematic issues with the dog ahead of time and target our training program to meet your facilities' need.

Even if the 100% consensus is present, please tell us about any specific concerns or potential drawbacks you anticipate because of the therapy dog's presence.

- Has your legal advisor, and/or your risk management department, explored the potential liability and determined appropriate insurance coverage for problems from any unexpected circumstances? Considerations would include bites, fright, objection, allergic reaction, or even something as mundane as a guest tripping and falling over the dog.

- Please list each function you expect the therapy dog to perform.

- Please briefly describe the general types of disabilities or difficulties for which your clients are treated, and/or the reasons for which they reside at your facility.

- What are the state and local codes for your facility regarding animals are concerned? In which areas (such as food preparation and serving) would the dog not be allowed by law?

- Your therapy dog will need to have a designated primary handler and a backup (in case of illness, absence, vacations, etc.) for each staffing shift at your facility. 100% coverage is necessary. Please list each shift and indicate the primary handler and the backup for each shift. Please include weekends. It will be necessary to arrange regular training time for all primary handlers, and to a lesser degree, the backup handlers.

Please list potential times the primary handlers would be available for training sessions.

Please list potential times the backup handlers would be available for training sessions.

- Do privately-owned therapy animals visit your facility at any time?

  If yes, are such animals required to have current certification from Therapy Dogs International?

  If yes, is it your expectation that these animals would interact with or be in contact with the resident dog?

- Do you anticipate the resident therapy dog leaving your facility/grounds for any official activities or outings?

  If yes, please briefly describe the type of activity or outing and the general type of location in which it would be held (park, shopping, etc.).

- Do you plan to use a professional groomer or are there facilities at your business for this purpose?

- What veterinarian do you plan to use?

- Who would be responsible for transporting the dog to a vet and caring for the dog in case of possible illness?

- Is one or more of your primary handlers able to care for the dog in his/her own home if a degree of illness or injury to the dog made resident work temporarily impossible or unadvised?

- Is there a fenced yard or a totally enclosed outdoor area in which the dog will be allowed periodic free time?

- Please describe your plan for providing regular exercise for the dog.

- Has the ongoing expense of a resident therapy dog been approved by your financial officer or budget committee? If not, do you anticipate any problem in covering this type of expense?

- Are there any other therapy animals in your facility? If so, please list name and species of each.

- Please describe the area in which the dog would be kenneled, and/or what part of your facility in which its work would be performed.

- Considering the likelihood of occasional clients who are allergic to dogs, or possibly phobic in some way, does the area described above have alternate or duplicate facilities for use by clients troubled by the dog's presence?

Chapter 14:

ASA Dogs

A what? For most readers, this is probably a new acronym, because it's one I made up myself during the last few years to apply to a certain kind of service dog. ASA stands for Assistive Search Alert dog. You won't find any legal recognition of the label. Though I'm aware of at least two other training programs that offer parallel services, so far as I know the term "ASA" is peculiar to Dogs for Disabled. While I am not devoting entire chapters to other specific types of service dogs, I believe an exception is warranted here because of the lack of reference material available for those contemplating such projects.

Assistive Search Alert dogs are regular service animals, trained and certified for public access with the disabled individual. The primary difference from other service animals is that they are trained to respond to the commands of a caregiver, for the benefit of the disabled person, rather than the disabled person himself. The difference in training is because the disabled individual cannot directly control the dog, and because the person with the disability is usually a child. So far, all but one of the ASA dogs have been trained for children who had autism. The one who did not have autism had a brain injury as a result of an accident. Therefore, in discussing the nature of ASA dogs and their jobs, I will refer to dogs as they have been trained to work with autistic children.

MULTIPLE FUNCTIONS

ASA dogs perform multiple jobs for their clients, as the name suggests—assisting, searching, and alerting.

Assistance

In certain situations, it is possible for a dog to assist a child in matters of focus and behavior. Many autistic children, for instance, are highly resentful of parental interference with their behavior. Although interference is often necessary, dogs can sometimes help a to allow parents' interaction to focus on more positive matters than a physical contest over agenda. For example, let's suppose a parent has a particular goal that a child will spend less time in a certain repetitive, self-stimulating, or destructive behavior—perhaps banging an object or a shoe (or a head) on the wall. For those who have children with autism, or know someone who does, it isn't any large surprise that the child probably won't calmly desist just because you ask. In fact, he might dive behind the sofa and continue the behavior where you cannot reach him. By the time you move the sofa to get yourself behind it, the child might be upstairs under the bed. Even if not, moving the sofa 15 times a day gets tiring. Add a dog with correct training to this equation and things might get simpler. Whatever the behavior, it's likely to be far less satisfying to the child if a dog is licking him and won't stop, or if the dog is persistently nudging and pushing him out from behind the sofa.

Please stay with me on this: I am *not* discussing a parental disciplinary tool. This is a technique that belongs in the behavior modification category. Many autistic children are highly stressed by constant adult interference with their actions. Some respond with less frustration or animosity to a dog than they would to a human. For those kids, reminders and prompts from a dog can remove the element of conflict with another person and improve the focus on the behavior itself.

Not to be disregarded is the aspect of a child wanting to manipulate. Though normal behavior from autistic children does not start with the desire to frustrate parents, that element can become a "way cool" by-product. Most autistic children are experiencing no problem with intelligence. Therefore it's pretty common for some behaviors to persist and grow merely because it causes excitement and entertainment. One of the best examples of this behavior I've seen was an eight-year-old girl who had a fascination for throwing things out any available window. Preferably breakable things. This had happened one day by accident and for reasons forever unknown, generated a fascination for watching things crash onto the sidewalk. Before the incorporation of the ASA dog, the parents had essentially three choices: never allow their daughter out of their sight, nail the windows shut, or put up with having multiple household items tossed onto the sidewalk—anything and everything small enough for the girl to handle. And she could undo any window-locking device faster than her parents.

The daughter's post-dog experiences with this hobby were slightly different: she couldn't get near a window because a big dog was always in the way. Piece of cake for the dog. Delightful for the parents who could avoid endless conflict and turn efforts toward more positive, desirable interactions with their daughter. In time, the girl stopped attempting The Window Routine. Whether she lost interest because of a lack of satisfaction or the cessation grew naturally out of her overall behavior modification program, no one really knew. The parents were merely grateful for the reduced legwork.

What behaviors an ASA dog can provide help with are highly specialized and must be evaluated according to the individual circumstances of any home. I've seen it work with incessant screaming, refusal to use furniture (that is, the child prefers being under the kitchen table to sitting at a chair at meals), and pulling off clothes. Only one problem area seems common to almost every home, which is that of the child having to be restrained in public. Many parents can testify that taking an autistic child to the grocery store is an exhausting experience for everyone. In many cases, constant contact with the child is required. Whether holding him by the hand or arm or otherwise, the restraint will leave the parent with one functioning hand, at best, with which to do normal business. Meanwhile the son or daughter constantly perceives that contact with Mom or Dad is restrictive.

In every case I've worked with so far, the child was quickly willing to accept the idea of walking with the dog via a wristband attachment to the dog's harness (equipped with an auditory purse-snatcher alarm that will sound off if loosened). This procedure is presented to the child as "walking your dog" rather than a matter of being restrained by the dog. The dog is actually controlled by the parent, with a regular leash and collar. Results: far greater freedom for the parent, greater independence and less frustration for the child. Plus again…the reduced conflict allowing both parties to focus on other factors. One of the clients had previously experienced many a footrace with their son, who would twist out of a grip and take off at the slightest opportunity. Again, this behavior probably began with the normal inclinations of autism to "fly solo" and avoid contact. In this particular case, there was little doubt the habit intensified because it became fun, causing excitement and effort from the parents: The Mom and Dad Show.

The presence of the dog eliminated the entire scenario. Mom and Dad were more comfortable, the son was more secure (whether he realized it or not), and public excursions became far more relaxed for all involved.

Search
The second function for an ASA dog is search. Any parent can tell you kids get gone faster than any organism on the planet, disability or no disability. The resulting challenges are enormous for parents of non-disabled children, but even more so for children with significantly increased vulnerability. Many children with autism are entirely non-verbal. If lost, they not only cannot ask for help, but they also may not be able to give any response to questions. In fact, it's fairly common that an autistic child might not *want* to be found—or even recognize that he is lost in the first place. He may bolt, then hide, making no response at all even to a nearby family member looking for him. This behavior is not about a poor family relationship or any such thing: it is merely the nature of the disability. And it is every parent's nightmare. A good dog, adequately trained in search functions, can greatly reduce the risk in any situation where the child might disappear.

While it's true that most police departments and/or emergency response teams already have trained search dogs, when a child goes missing, the difference between safety and disaster can be a matter of moments. Consider the value of a dog who is already on the scene, with appropriate training, and a desire to locate a child that he already considers "his." Not to mention that hiding from Mom and Dad isn't going to work if a dog is the one doing the looking.

Alert

The third function of an ASA dog is alerting. Much in the manner of a hearing assistance dog, an ASA dog can be trained to provide a signal if a child leaves, or appears to be attempting to leave, the house or yard. While I would stress that the dog is not a baby-sitter or a substitute for adequate human supervision of a disabled child, he can be a great backup plan. Parents do need to sleep occasionally. Door alarms sometimes fail. An autistic child is often very capable of finding the hidden key to that deadbolt. It's not always possible to secure totally every access to the house. If everyone is outside, even in a fenced yard, a 20-second distraction to the parent can provide enough time for a child to scale a fence and disappear. It may not be a frequent occurrence, but one time is all it takes. An alert from a vigilant dog can provide much peace of mind to the parent: an additional safety margin for a child who cannot possibly understand the danger he'd face by leaving.

DEMANDING ROLE

If ASA dogs sound too good to be true—don't worry, they're not. Like everything else we've discussed in this book, they are a tool, not a pill. They can help, but they are certainly not a fool-proof, automatic fix. The main drawback is that I know of no other type of training that places such enormous demands on the handling skill of the parent. Much of the training absolutely must take place in the home, and unless a trainer can move in for several months, much of it will have to be done by the parents. Furthermore, this is an exercise more in shaping a dog's behavior than it is teaching certain commands and responses. The dogs must take a huge amount of initiative, and ultimately be able to work independently, without any guidance or cues, for the majority of their functions.

Careful Selection

As with resident therapy dogs, the selection of an ASA dog is undoubtedly the most critical aspect of the training/placement process. The dog's inclinations to provide the needed assistance have to be "hard-wired." The constant alertness, the high drive to maintain the pack, the desire to contain and supervise the child, commitment to search for a missing member—these are characteristics that have, so far, caused me to go shopping for candidates exclusively among the herding breeds. Thus far, German Shepherds have provided the highest percentage of candidates. Among the herding breeds, their particular style of herding is related to containment and boundaries. Among breeders and professionals, this is referred to as "tending" herding, rather than the "fetch and gather" function seen at typical herding trials. In the herding role for which they were developed, German Shepherds form a "living fence" between a herd of livestock and any area where the animals are not supposed to be. This natural behavior applies itself extremely well to natural watchfulness of children in a home setting.

Non-Aggressive

It's also important to consider that any suitable ASA dog must have an extremely relaxed temperament. Herding breeds, and German Shepherds in particular, normally have natural protective aggression in their personalities—especially where "their" children are concerned. While this cannot be entirely eliminated in any dog, any ASA dog absolutely must have a far-below-average tendency for interpreting threats. Trainers often refer to this characteristic as a dog who has a "high threshold." Whatever you prefer to call it, an ASA dog *cannot* be trigger happy. Far too many herding breed dogs, who would otherwise be very capable of this job, have a level of protective aggression that would make them unsafe to perform this job in public settings. For a systematic approach to evaluate character and temperament in a German Shepherd, see Appendix A.

Early Placement

For me, personally, the difficulty in finding good ASA candidates is what finally turned me to a breeding program, rather than looking for dogs from among my normal sources. It is almost imperative that the dog be placed in the home earlier than would be the norm for service dogs. Proper exposure to the family and proper development of behavior patterns in the dog demand early placement—if not in actual puppyhood, at least during canine adolescence. Given the difficulty of predicting a mature dog's character when starting with a pup of unknown background, I believe starting with a known quantity is essential. Even dealing with experienced breeders, I have found it extraordinarily difficult to find the exact blend of traits needed in the adult dogs, let alone have any depth of field to choose from among the pups. Lastly, the number of breeders selling older pups of several months is far fewer than those selling babies. Again, possible? Yes. A much higher number of work-hours to pull off? Also yes. I am fairly well convinced that if this type of service dog becomes more common in the future, it will be through programs or individuals who have established a reliable breeding line of suitable candidates.

Getting Help

Finally, be sure that adding an ASA dog to any home is a matter that calls for more complete and experienced evaluation than is possible from the parent and trainer alone. I recommend, without exception, consulting a behavioral health professional for advice on practicality, safety, and potential outcome. In my very first experience placing a dog with an autistic child, I was fortunate enough to work with a mother who happened to have a Ph.D. in

Education of Exceptional Children. Though her goals for her daughter and her companion dog were very different from the ASA dogs described here, I was able to learn a great deal from this insightful woman and have incorporated many of her suggestions and guidelines into the current efforts. One element she managed to din into my head was to heed advice from those who have adequate professional skill working with the widely-varied and highly sensitive nature of autism.

POTENTIAL VARIATIONS

As an aside, let me stress an important point. I am aware that many people are dealing with a disability other than autism in a family member, in circumstances where an ASA dog might be desirable. These are disabilities of a mental nature, rather than physical, such as the brain injury referred to at the beginning of this chapter, or possibly Alzheimers or Down Syndrome. While I personally believe there is a great future for this type of service dog, I caution that many of the aspects are yet unexplored. Any effort toward training and placing a dog to do such a job will involve experimental technique. Possibly even trial and error attempts. As defined in Chapter 7, the specific tasks an ASA dog must perform are mostly Category 3—perhaps reinforceable in training, but not necessarily in reality.

EXPERIENCE REQUIRED

Apart from assessing the amount of effort you are willing to commit to a trial project, be aware such a project is not a place for novice training efforts. Such scenarios are not appropriate for trainers or for families to undertake without much prior experience. Any trainer or group working with this type of project should already to be completely fluent in the more common venues of training assistance dogs and also search dogs. Expertise in these fields must be a given—readily available in order to address the additional complications of incorporating a mental disability into the training process. The safety of all involved, human and canine, should be of paramount importance. Again, input from a professional in the field of mental health should be an absolute requirement.

Caregivers will need to devote a great deal of thought to how much effort and expense they are willing to expend on a training effort of uncertain outcome. Additionally, I have found the expense to be astronomical, based purely on the number of training hours, and often the resulting travel, required to make the ASA dogs effective. In hopes of adding perspective, I close this chapter with the personal testimony of a parent who found herself in exactly this situation.

Don't Give Up

Kelly Capers, who has an autistic son, was our very first client in the ASA training endeavor. For almost a year, Kelly made an all-day round trip every week to the Dogs for Disabled kennel to gain the training and handling expertise necessary for a project that was completely experimental at that time. The Capers family endured our greenness, our delays, our screwups, and even our juvenile level of enthusiasm over the wonderful results. I salute their commitment and dedication to their son and also their extraordinary efforts to provide him greater independence and safety. Kelly relates the following about their experience in obtaining—and retaining—an ASA dog named Larissa.

"As the parent of a special needs child, I have been willing to try anything to offer my son a better quality of life. As a lifelong dog person, it was inevitable that I would be curious about using a service dog with my unique child. When my son, who has autism, was four, I began what turned out to be a long and frustrating search for a service dog. Because I had volunteered with a service dog organization, I knew that canines can be taught to do remarkable things. I also knew that it took a special dog with special training to meet the needs of its partner. Beyond that, I knew that because my son was mentally challenged and not physically disabled our needs would be unique. I was prepared to be a guinea pig for anyone willing to work with us.

"I was not prepared for the magnitude of the search for help. For two years I called every organization that I learned of asking two important questions. 'Do you work with children?' and 'Do you work with individuals with autism?' If the answer to the first question wasn't 'No,' then the answer to the second was. I got every kind of response imaginable. Some people felt it was a good idea, but they didn't know how to accomplish the task. Some people bluntly told me that dogs could never be trained to work with autistic people. Few saw the value in a mother using a service dog with a child and one told me flat out that I wanted a surrogate mother for my child because I didn't want to be responsible for him. While many others were sympathetic, no one was willing to work with an autistic child.

"I began to realize that if I were going to try working with a service dog I would have to train one myself. I felt confident that I could do the training, but I had no idea what traits to look for in a good dog. I also had no idea where to begin teaching commands for the tasks I wanted performed. So I changed the focus of my search. I no longer hunted for an organization to provide me with a trained dog. I now was looking for information on how to train.

"I began this search in the library. The right book, I believed, could tell me how to choose and train a service dog. Yet, before I had begun, my search for information hit a brick wall. I found not one book on training service dogs. Although I found many books on canine behavior, there was nothing to tell me how to find or train a dog to work with the disabled. Even organizations and individuals famous for training service dogs had no manual or publication to offer advice.

"So once again I began calling service dog organizations. At that time, I found two who offered the kind of training I needed. The one closest to my home was a three-hour drive away. The training took nine months. From the beginning, the project was an experiment. I was working with people who had never attempted to train a dog for the tasks I needed. However, they saw nothing as impossible and were willing to try the experiment. An ongoing project, there have been many ups and downs.

"I was fortunate to find a training opportunity within driving distance of my home. Because there are few organizations that offer this training, people who want to work with service dogs often have to be prepared to travel great distances staying in hotels or dormitories during the training. Some programs are intense short-term programs. Others offer classes once a week and last several months. Either way, the training takes a great deal of time and requires a serious commitment. Training, working with, and living with [an ASA dog] is ongoing and never ending, but it is worth the effort to me to offer my son even an ounce of independence that he might not otherwise have.

"Although we don't use a service dog in the traditional sense, Larissa helps our family daily by knowing where Jack is at all times. She counts heads during the night, and I know that if anyone were missing, she'd go nuts. In public she is valuable to him by offering him a guide to walk independently. He is 11 now and doing much better about walking alone without holding one of our hands. When we are somewhere in a crowd, which can still be a daunting experience, Larissa allows him to walk alone without holding our hands. That's important to a preteen boy, even one who is autistic. Jack is also able to play in the yard alone for the same reason. I can't just send him outside without watching him, but with Larissa with him, I can allow him to play in the yard without someone staring at him every second.

"Having an ASA dog has made a huge difference in how we live our lives. Larissa has truly changed our lives."

—Kelly Capers
August 2003

SUGGESTED READING

A Child's Best Friend. 20 May 2005.
   <autism.about.com/cs/serviceanimals/l/blsvcdog.htm>

Adams, Cindy L. and Kristen E. Burrows. *Evaluating the Benefits of Service Dogs for Children with Autism Spectrum Disorder.* 2003 20 May 2005. <www.nsd.on.ca/research.htm>

Chapter 15:

Programs and Opinions

 If you're reading for information only and prefer to avoid opinions, you might want to skip this chapter entirely. If you're interested in some personal conclusions based on a decade-plus of work with service dog programs, read on. Despite frequent use of the terms "programs" and "trainers," I'm not sure they are the best word choices (though they're certainly the common ones). After all, every service dog program has trainers, and presumably any good trainer uses a program of some sort. But those are semantic differences. As mentioned in Chapter 2, I use "programs" in reference to an organization, not to a trainer's choice of protocol. Service dog training programs are usually non-profit corporations whose entire purpose is to provide service dogs to clients. Among the total number of finished service dogs placed with disabled clients in the US, these organizations are responsible for the largest percentage.

More than a decade of work with a typical program has left me with some rather definite views on their strengths and weaknesses. While I am fully in support of the profound efforts of many people (after all, I'm one of the many), I also believe the system, has two pretty serious problems. The problems are related, but distinct.

ACCOUNTABILITY

Generally speaking, many programs lack accountability. Whether you are a client or a sponsor, I urge you to give serious thought to how a program demonstrates its quality. Too many don't really do so at all. An adequate demonstration is not a matter of a few parlor tricks during a rotary club luncheon, nor even a videotaped demonstration (though they are often helpful) in which dogs and footage can be selectively shown.

Almost every competent, experienced service dog trainer will agree that the "industry" needs a standard of excellence. The subsequent array of disagreement and resistance is more about our collective fear, as trainers, of being monitored by people who know far less about training than we do—or who are more interested in the corporate image than in practical success. Assistance Dogs International has taken some superb steps to give clients a framework for assessment, and also a forum for complaints. However, I believe we—"we" being the people who make up the industry—are still missing a some critical factors. I believe the quality of the product should be made more readily evident to the general public, which includes sponsors, clients, and potential people for either category.

Dog training is not an exact science. One cannot measure and quantify results exactly the same way you can with other non-profit causes, such as disease treatment, feeding the hungry, or providing financial relief to disaster areas. For many groups, success is obvious: either the desired action happens or it does not. Even in the guide dog subset of service dog work, the specific results are far more observable and far more concrete than that of dogs trained for wider-ranging disabilities. My personal position (though certain to be intensely unpopular) is that an accountability system should be required by law. It is true that the widely varying range of disabilities among clients prevents any realistic standardized test of *all* service dog functions. However, a standard of minimum performance is an idea whose time has come. Independently-evaluated performance would go a long way toward sorting out confusion about which programs are turning out quality service dogs…and which are not. Far too few training programs subject their finished product (the dogs…not the clients!) to independent review.

CHECKS AND BALANCES

In many programs the same person or small group is responsible for fund raising, operational strategy, and quality control, which is a perfectly acceptable strategy if you choose to do it with your own money. Most sole-proprietorships do just that. However, I believe dealing with publicly-supported charities calls for more accountability. We know training methodology varies considerably. A stonewall answer of "Our policy is_____ , *period*" does not go far enough. Should sponsors and clients listen? In Chapter 4, I've already suggested some minimum standards to impose on private training efforts. But most large programs don't plan to implement such practices anytime soon. In many cases, neither supporters nor clients have a defined method to review and critique the program's product, before or after their participation. That is, I believe, what needs to change.

Client Privacy

Please allow me to be clear on a critically important point: I am not recommending that clients be pressured into the spotlight for purposes of evaluating the success of contributions. If individual clients wish to share their stories, through a medium of their own choosing, that's a very personal decision and is certainly fine with me. Programs and sponsors will both be grateful for the public feedback. But for any program to require such, or even imply that doing so will make any difference in the client's status, is highly inappropriate and possibly illegal.

Reliable Training

However, when it comes to the issue of the dogs and the quality of training, I have no patience—and no mercy. I am near the conclusion that most people who have ever taught a dog to sit consider themselves a "trainer." Charitable funding, the savings of people on disability income, insurance payouts, and more recently even state funding are all going toward paying for these service dogs. I consider it ludicrous to allow dogs to exit training with no standard, required method of ensuring even a basic level of quality.

Independent Evaluation

As I have said in previous chapters, I believe someday, something in the way of the requirements currently outlined by Assistance Dogs International will be legally required. I hope so. ADI is addressing a need of enormous importance: applying a quality standard to service dog training and use. ADI's advocacy of a Minimum Performance Test is superb. In my private dream world, I would love to see the standard taken one step further and have the test evaluated not by program personnel, but by an independent judge from the regularly-approved panels of the AKC, UKC, USA, or WDA. The procedure would retain privacy, yet ensure an independent evaluation by someone already qualified to judge fluency of basic training. A Minimum Performance Test reviews not only part of a dog's specific job description, but also the quality of the instruction to the client. If more trainers and programs were willing to take this step, the judge's scoresheet—identified only by the dog's microchip number—could be available in all its detailed, successful glory for both sponsors and potential clients to see. Sponsors would be able to see specifics about where and to what their dollars were going. Clients could get a far more realistic idea of what lies ahead of them.

NATIONAL REGISTRATION

Beyond a greater degree of independent assessment (or perhaps I should say "in addition to"), my personal opinion is that there should be a national registration of all service animals, including at least the following components:

- Medical verification of disability
- Identification and signature of the trainer
- Microchip identification of the animal
- For dogs, certificate from the American Kennel Club, United Kennel Club, United Schutzhund Clubs of America, or Working Dog Association acknowledging the dog's completion of a Companion Dog test or title under the trainer's handling. In the case of non-canine service animals, an appropriate, nationally-recognized expert panel should indicate a reliable training-safety test.

I am not under any delusions about the popularity of my opinion, but I still believe strongly in the need. A national registration would certainly *not* solve all quality-related problems, because it would not address performance of the widely-varied service dog functions. But it *would* help eliminate imposters and demonstrate at least a degree of basic safety and control in public, which is considerably more than we have now.

Possible Venue

How could we possibly implement such a national registration? At this time the concept is so far from reality, the only answers are those in brainstorming mode. But it seems to me the logical solution would be through states' Departments of Motor Vehicles, via driver's licenses or general identification cards. A parallel concept is already in place: there is a procedure for obtaining a permit to park in slots reserved for people with disabilities. For service dog use, the only requirement should be a licensed physician's verification of the presence of a disability—the particulars of the disability being none of anyone else's business. The dog would then be referred to on the individual's card, much like is done with corrective lenses.

Objections

Over the years I've presented my ideas on national registration in quite a few places, but have only rarely found a receptive audience. I have, on the other hand, been given many rebuttals about why it's not necessary—or possibly even a violation of civil rights. Among the objections are that either national registration and/or independent evaluation would be an additional expense, too time consuming, too complicated, too intrusive, or an ineffective solution for all potential problems. I've been told that other programs' testing procedures are more extensive or better. Privacy is too important. If you name the objection, I've probably already heard it. Even most of the national advocacy groups that I otherwise support do not consider it necessary—or perhaps even actually detrimental.

Even so, none of the above makes a shred of difference to my personal opinion. I fail to see how it would compromise privacy. Individual physicians are the only ones who would know even the nature of a disability, and it ought to be safe to assume they already have such information. People with disabilities normally must go through a very similar process merely to obtain the right to park in a Handicapped Parking Area. Does it seem reasonable that the permissions process for taking a carnivore in public be at least the equivalent of a parking sticker?

Over the years I have spent considerable time, effort, and money in varying roles—trainer, client, program director, and even sponsor. Having also had considerable interaction with people in parallel roles in other places, nothing is going to convince me that the American service dog industry has anything remotely approaching a quality standard. People *are* trying. Groups *are* trying. Efforts *are* honorable. But we are *not* there yet.

Consistency

I believe financial sponsors, the public, and clients deserve at least a basic demonstration of training and safety. In order to be worth the name, a standard has to apply the same rules to everyone. Quite a few large programs keep their kennels and even their training sessions open to the public. That is a wonderful practice and I applaud it heartily. If I had a million dollars to give to a program, it would almost certainly go to such a place. But even open-observation policies stop short of providing independent evaluation and measuring *every* dog by the same yardstick.

I'll take this one step further. Some programs are already implementing the outside evaluations described above. Dogs for Disabled is one of them. I'll let the other programs speak for themselves at a time and place of their own choosing. Dogs For Disabled adopted the evaluation system suggested here in the latter part of 2003. From that point forward, trainers must handle the dogs during a companion dog test as described in Chapter 4. These tests will be advertised to clients and sponsors as much as possible *before* the event—not merely after completion. To the greatest extent possible, the candidates will be publicly identified as Dogs for Disabled trainees. If the various organizations, such as the American Kennel Club, ever choose to modify their policies and allow identifying equipment on service dogs, then our dogs will wear Dogs for Disabled vests while actually performing the tests. In my private dream world, I dare to hope that someday the AKC might implement separate classes specifically to exhibit the skills of service dogs.

In another outside evaluation, Dogs for Disabled clients, with their dogs, complete their Minimum Performance Test with no audience allowed except the judge, unless the client requests that someone else be present. Anonymous scoresheets are available to sponsors and clients. We hope—in the same way it is the hope of those who established ADI—that eventually this kind of voluntary review will minimize problems and impose higher quality control on the entire industry.

ENORMOUS EFFORTS

At the beginning of this chapter, I referred to two major problems among service dog programs. If independent quality review is one, what is the other? I'll get to that in just a moment, right after I tell you what the second issue is *not,* and it's *not* a lack of dedication on the part of the majority of program personnel.

Dedicated Trainers

For those of you who might assume I am the Ralph Nader of the service dog world, always ready to pounce on the big, bad, ineffective programs…you're wrong. If there is a more difficult profession with less recognition and financial reward, I'm not sure what it might be. I suppose probably the clergy or police is far worse. However, the majority of trainers and programs are doing the best they know how to do, because they believe in the need for their work. It is not by any means the sincerity of their effort that should be questioned.

More often than clients might believe, trainers' hands are tied by boards of directors who care less for effectiveness than public appeal. More often than decorum allows us to relate, clients spend their first year complaining because they don't have a dog yet, and the rest of the dog's life complaining about the dog, the trainers, the cost, and the problems. To say the trainers' jobs can be thankless does not make the raw beginning of an accurate commentary.

Limited Budgets

It's also frustrating, but equally true, that financial limitations simply do not allow programs to respond to every needful situation they encounter. For instance, many times we have been approached by people who already had service dogs and then saw a Dogs For Disabled client/dog team working together. They realize it's possible to have more than they're getting from their own dog. Thus, they call and ask for help in re-training. We used to undertake some of these projects. Then we quit. For those who have a genuine need and a good dog, please see the section in Chapter 10 about training "pre-owned" dogs. For the rest, we learned by the school of very hard kicks in our derrieres, that a substantial percentage of these people were defiant graduates, or even dropouts, of other programs. Their problems arose precisely because they would not follow instructions or cooperate with trainers. While clients have a right—and a responsibility—to choose the trainer who is the best option and who most fully meets their needs, they also have a moral obligation to cooperate with the training protocol and follow the long-term outline for succeeding with their dogs. They chose it, didn't they?

Necessary Red Tape

The ill-reputed "bureaucracy" of most service dog programs usually grows from the same place it does in any company of long standing: the desire to avoid repeating errors. On this subject, probably 90% of the scenarios will find me on the side of the trainer. I'm a great fan of the old southern saying, "There ain't no education in the second kick of a mule." This mode of thought leads us by degrees into the second major dilemma faced by many programs—and it has nothing to do with dedication or desire to produce quality dogs. It has everything to do with funding.

INVERSE RATIOS

Training programs are fun and exciting in their infancy. Well-trained dogs are making huge differences in the lives of clients. Everyone is thrilled and well-motivated. Obtaining funding is a snap, since the dogs are few, overhead is low, and sponsors are excited to have something local. At the far end of the spectrum, you have a handful of well-established programs with a full-time operational staff, perhaps a breeding program, and a large number of available trainers. The distance between those two places—the tiny and the large—is more than a gap. It's a chasm into which many otherwise very capable programs fall and vanish forever.

Success Increases Demand

Business decisions, leadership, future planning…yes, they all play a role, as they do in any organization in the world. But there is a slightly more subtle issue that's often not well-recognized. Baseline growth of graduates strains operational resources. A Catch-22 forms: the most successful trainers face the largest difficulty. Every client's need for support lasts the lifetime of the dog, which is something that is hard to correctly appreciate from the starting line. Show me an innovative, dedicated trainer who gets the job done, and five years from now I'll probably show you an overwhelmed trainer who needs extra staff just to keep up with past trainees. Everybody is terrifically impressed with the good trainer's dogs, right? So everybody wants to use that trainer, right? The more dogs he or she (or any particular group) trains, the more they have out there as "graduates." Trainers reach their time limits. Volunteers burn out. Board members turn into "bored" members and go home. Whatever your capabilities as an individual or small group, you will eventually exceed them unless you continue to expand the operational base along with your number of graduates. But doing so is trickier than it might sound.

Increased Growth

For programs that survive the first decade of operation, yet another logistical crush awaits. Somewhere around their eighth or tenth year, many of the clients from the early years begin needing new dogs. Second placements converge with all the existing first-time clients, and the case load becomes staggering. At the time this book heads for press, more than one of the better-known service dog programs in the country are currently able to serve only their existing clients. Funding and personnel are simply not available to expand services to any new people, regardless of the level of need. It's a tough dilemma.

Many clients are on disability income and have little discretionary cash to meet ongoing training expenses. However, a large number of sponsors do not want to fund general operating expenses. Specific, urgent needs have sexier appeal, generating more public attention and making nicer pictures. Unfortunately, it's often a losing game for those who were last year's great stories. I know of no magic formula to fill this gap except for an enormous amount of legwork and enough expense built into the cost of each dog to cover some general expenses.

Compatible Solutions

I also consider this operating-expense dilemma to be an argument for the concept of quality testing. I would love to urge sponsors and volunteers to focus more effort on supporting operational expense. But many sponsors are wary for precisely the reasons I've already outlined: they want to know that the money is being used effectively. Restricting the use of donated funds to a specific purpose allows them to know what is happening to the money—that the dog is actually getting trained and someone is being helped. I believe that a solution for our first dilemma—a parade of finished dogs successfully completing independent evaluations—would aid the second dilemma of giving sponsors a means of evaluation.

This resulting burnout scenario—full of exhausted volunteers and underpaid staff—is very real to many programs. It's just often swept under the rug for fear of being misunderstood or of harming future contributions. Who wants to be known as "maxed out?" I know of multiple situations in which exactly this problem has happened to very competent training groups—programs with incredibly successful dogs who grew, and grew…and *grew,* but the base of operational support did not keep pace. Eventually every such group hits the proverbial wall. The result will be a lot of (rightly) frustrated clients and some seriously overstretched trainers and board members. They are struggling for day-to-day functionality, with no clue whether or not help will arrive in time to keep them from disappearing into the abyss. Even if the help arrives, it may take them many years to regroup.

If you are a sponsor (and even a client paying for his own dog is to some extent "sponsoring"), I would urge you to consider the broad scope of responsibility in training that extends far beyond immediate placement expenses. Please consider supporting the general operating expenses of training programs, as well as specific needs. However, I will also suggest sponsors give some thought to an observable standard of performance as a prerequisite for your support.

THE CHALLENGE WE FACE

The number of folks with disabilities is not getting any smaller. Recognition of assistance dog utility is growing. Compared to the guide dog industry, for example, we are only in our infancy. Any problems that have arisen since 1990 are likely to be magnified in the future. I doubt there is any service dog trainer in the United States who would not hastily assure you that training for disability assistance utterly obliterates other types of dog training for pure satisfaction, worthwhile results, and extreme need.

But the industry faces the exact same problem many businesses and government departments face today: insufficient financial resources. The difference is that we cannot rely on increased retail sales or more congressional votes. Most of us are non-profit groups and we survive because of others' approval and help. Regardless of what is or isn't true, what we do or don't know about our dogs and clients…for both sponsors and our clients, their perception is their reality. Speaking to my fellow trainers and program members, let's assume the burden of proof and show the world, in a concrete, objective way, that what we're doing is not only worthwhile but reliable.

Appendix A:

When Personality Meets Character

If you're going to use a Golden Retriever or a Labrador for your service dog, you can probably safely skip this appendix, though depending on your level of interest in canine psychology, you might find it interesting to read anyway. Temperament considerations are important in any dog, but possibly even more so with certain breeds or types, most notably some of the herding and guarding breeds, such as the German Shepherd Dogs, Belgian Shepherds, Malinois, Dobermans, Rottweilers, Boxers, and quite a few others.

Though I believe that most people needing a service dog do best with retrievers, there are certainly situations that favor use of different breeds. For instance, my own special area of interest in service dog training is one of them (ASA dogs, as discussed in Chapter 14). So far, I have discovered no breed better suited to that particular interest than the German Shepherd. Unfortunately, German Shepherds rank in the top echelons of breeds plagued by nervousness, instability, and fear biting. That fact creates an enormous responsibility for me to be extremely comprehensive in temperament evaluations. The same applies to anyone—whether trainer or client or both—who is adamant about using a breed characterized by natural protectiveness. If you plan to be safe and effective, you have homework to do.

The process I use for evaluating breeding stock and/or working dogs is far too extensive to detail here. Much of it wouldn't apply directly to the discussion of temperament soundness anyway because it is for a very specialized type of work. But some of it does. In a few paragraphs, we'll delve into a soundness-evaluating process used by many breeders. You might want to go get a cup of coffee…we're going to get technical on a fairly complex topic. The material covered in this appendix is about a procedure that originated in the early 1900s as a means of testing working ability in German Shepherds. The superb results caused its use to spread widely among many different working breeds.

For the most part, I've tried to avoid too much technicality, but this is one time it's necessary. I would be remiss to exclude the details, because I doubt there is any temperament test more misunderstood, more controversial—or more valuable. Those who understand the value have used the test for decades to evaluate character and working potential in many breeds. What test? I wish there were another term to use, since the most common term, in and of itself, causes confusion. The term is "Schutzhund," which is German and translates literally to "protection dog." I consider even the translation to be a misnomer, since the process consists of three parts—none of which is actual protection work in the same sense a police dog or personal protection dog is trained. Schutzhund, in its original purpose, was a beautifully-developed means of weeding dogs out of the gene pool who showed weak character, nervous temperament, or unwillingness to work. In the hands of an experienced trainer, it can still do exactly that! Furthermore, because of the immense challenge and the excellent development of relationship between handler and dog, the term is also used by various groups in different countries who do "Schutzhund" as a competitive sport. Crossing the line into competition, however, Schutzhund, like any other dog sport, takes on a natural limitation regarding what you see on the competition field itself. Again, such a concept goes straight back to the discussion in Chapter 5 about the fact that competitions reward training skill as well as canine nature. Unless you know the training *process,* you don't necessarily have complete information about the dog.

CONTEXT

Let's go back to the individual breeds for a moment. When discussing breed variations in Chapter 9, we looked briefly at why some dogs were developed to have more natural suspicion and aloofness than others. (Remember the difference between personality inclinations and temperament issues?) While these breeds are excellent workers for many jobs, the inclination to be suspicious is still there—granted, in varying degrees—regardless of the dog's soundness or unsoundness of temperament. Such breeds were most definitely developed for willingness to stand and fight not only against predators, but people as well. They had to. The protective, fighting capability was not about sport, ego, or image; it was part of the dogs' job, part of their purpose for living and part of what kept their owners living. But that historical willingness remains of huge importance when considering which of them would be appropriate for today's service dog work. Having looked at the "why" they were developed to be the way they were, let's look at the "how."

HISTORY

The Schutzhund testing format began in connection with the founding of the German Shepherd breed. It has been commonly

used ever since in the evaluation and training of many breeds and also mixed breeds, throughout many countries, such as discussed in the book *So That Others May Live,* by Caroline Hebard, who is well-known for her efforts with Search and Rescue (SAR) work.[1] Almost all the German Shepherd breeding stock in the various guide dog programs originated in Schutzhund-screened dogs.
The first overall purpose is to prove soundness of temperament, willingness to work, and absence of inappropriate aggression. The second is to develop an accurate picture of any participating dog's potential (whether high or low) for different kinds of jobs, such as search and rescue, search for objects (such as drugs or explosives), and police patrol work.

At one time the "conditions" for proving temperament soundness were even more stringent than many of us would like to think about. Early in the years of the development of German Shepherds, the breed's founder, Captain Max von Stephanitz, began to perceive problems in the soundness of many of the dogs being exhibited for the national championship—the *Sieger*—and began to take a strong approach to correcting the problem. Various stories circulate about the 1930 championship when he chose the victor, Herold aus der Niederlausitz, by challenging the dog with a 1,200-lb. horse. Stephanitz rode in increasingly smaller circles around the dog and actually attempted to jump the horse over the dog to see if he would bolt or be afraid. Herold (whose handler was out of sight) stood up to the test on his own and consequently was awarded the Sieger title.[2]

Keep in mind that today's canines from protectively-inclined breeds are descended from dogs with similar personalities! The

---

[1] *So That Others May Live,* by Frank Whittmore with Caroline Hebard (Bantam, 1996).
[2] For an interesting historical read about this entire process, see *The German Shepherd in Word and Picture,* by Max von Stephanitz (Hoflin Pub Ltd, Rep. edition, 1994).

personalities are mostly still there; what you want to know is what has happened to their soundness through the interim generations. It's intensely critical to know each individual dog's degree of both self-confidence and sensitivity to perceived threats. Trainers must select with extreme care and intense scrutiny.

THE PROCESS

We're about to take a look at how a trainer conducts that evaluation and then draw some parallels to how a service dog trainer might put the same type of tests to use for himself, in a slightly different way. Please keep in mind that it's not possible to completely explain the details here in this appendix—in other words, this is *not* a "how to" manual, but a brief overview of the Schutzhund evaluation process. First, let's establish two extremely important concepts.

Misunderstandings

In most service dog circles today, admitting you participate in any form of Schutzhund process is roughly equivalent to entering a restaurant and loudly announcing you have a case of contagious hemorrhagic fever. Even as I type, I can hear the distant *whir* of computers all across America firing up to verbally peel the hide off of this clueless, dangerous, obnoxious, so-called trainer who is recommending such technique. In the minds of many people Schutzhund routines have become synonymous with "attack training." And more dangerous foolishness goes on in the name of "attack training" or "protection training" than could possibly be documented in one book. However, it is completely incorrect to categorize Schutzhund testing as an unsafe practice or as a technique that creates or increases a dog's tendency to attack a human. It does not! Nothing will budge me from the position that negative reactions to Schutzhund evaluations—though arising from the best of intentions—stem from misunderstanding or simply a lack of information.

The value of three-phase work (Schutzhund) as a character test is difficult to overstate. Many breeders and trainers of various herding or guarding breeds have learned the value of testing dogs this way; as a result, a large percentage of them consider it essentially unethical to bypass the process. They hold that position because they know they can get information about their dogs through Schutzhund testing that simply cannot be had any other way. If you face the prospect of choosing your own candidate for service training, I would urge you to keep an open mind, and read on. If you never have a single thing to do with a Schutzhund evaluation, the information here could possibly still give you some new and interesting perspective on assessing a dog's temperament.

Titles Versus Testing

Second, let's not confuse using Schutzhund technique to *evaluate* dogs with actually training dogs to perform in a competition and obtain a title. Various sporting or breeders' associations around the world have formal training groups, "clubs," and associated trials through which the members' dogs compete for Schutzhund as a sport or as an exhibit of soundness. That is not my point or my focus in this appendix, nor what I am advocating for service dog training. My primary goal is to help someone who is considering a classically protective breed understand at least a little about how versatile working dogs were developed and tested. To understand what the test shows is to understand how it can be used to evaluate dogs for more than one type of job. A great deal can be learned about a given dog's soundness, initiative, and level (or lack) of aggression. It's the information we're after, not the title. But…

exactly what information? I'm so glad you asked! Now that we know what I am *not* talking about, let's move on to the specifics.

THE TITLE

Let's back up for a moment and focus for a bit on what the process actually contains. It should be noted at this point that before a dog is eligible to try for an actual Schutzhund title with any competition group, he must pass the Begleithund (BH) temperament test, as described in Chapter 4. After that qualification, to obtain an actual Schutzhund *title*, a dog must perform acceptably in each of the following three tests, all conducted on the same day, one right after another.

Tracking

The dog must closely and carefully follow a non-visible scent trail of several hundred yards. The "track" contains multiple corners and several articles which must be located and indicated to the handler. No deviation and little distraction is permitted, including that from bystanders, wildlife, other dogs, or the environment in general. Though the dog is usually on a line, he does not have to be. Some dogs perform the entire tracking phase at full liberty. Either way, the handler is strictly limited in how closely he may approach the dog and how much he is allowed to speak, nor may the dog return to the handler for any additional direction. (A dog of desirable service dog temperament would quickly and easily learn to follow the scent and be reliable about taking the initiative to do so, regardless of surroundings. He will not feel the need to "check in" with his handler, but will work at the distance with confidence and complete the task without continual urging.)

Obedience

While off leash at all times, the dog must perform a heeling pattern, move among a group of people, remain completely nonreactive to gunfire while heeling, do retrieves and jumps, respond to commands while in motion and at a distance, and hold a down/stay with the handler out of sight while another dog does the obedience exercises. (A good service dog candidate would respond with enthusiasm, but not hyperactivity, to the obedience commands, again regardless of the surrounding circumstances. He will be relaxed and comfortable whether he and the handler are close or apart and will not take advantage of any distance from the handler to shirk a task. Evaluation should focus on the consistency, rather than the quickness, of the dog's response.)

Protection

The dog must participate in a specific, tightly-structured routine involving both his handler and a stranger (also called a "helper," since his job is to help a judge evaluate the dog's temperament during the test) who wears a large burlap sleeve. The dog is off-leash at all times and must leave the handler, go to the area indicated, and search for the stranger. When he finds him, the dog is not allowed to touch him in any way. He must only alert and bark. When the time comes that he is allowed to grab the sleeve, he must maintain his grip on the sleeve, and only the sleeve, even when being physically threatened right into his face and struck on the ribs with a light stick. The dog has to release the sleeve on command from his handler, again, not touching the stranger in any way after letting go. The dog has to fend off a full-fledged attack by the stranger on himself and on his handler. This "attack" happens at a great distance from the handler—and the dog must pass right by the neutral judge before engaging the stranger's sleeve. Again, the dog must stop and let go on command from a distance, then must stay by the handler's side as he escorts the stranger in a simulated apprehension. Both human and dog return to the judge without touching or bothering the stranger in any way; the dog must stay obedient to the handler the entire time. (A good service dog candidate would consider this entire scenario to be nothing but a fun game about a desirable toy, demonstrating his willingness to work with a complete stranger, unaffected by new circumstances and remaining completely biddable to the handler.)

THE EVALUATION

All right, if that's what's involved in a Schutzhund title, then what's different about an "evaluation?" The primary difference is that a classic evaluation has to do with the dog's initial reactions and attitude, particularly when distractions and extraneous pressure come to bear. That's fairly self-explanatory in tracking and obedience: does the dog (or does he not) remain focused, steady, and reliable? How much training and enforcement do you have to do and how much focus is a spontaneous offer from the dog? However, this observation of initial tendency is even more important where involvement with the "helper" is concerned, because it demonstrates not only the dog's initiative, but also his sensitivity to perceiving a threat and how he reacts to a perceived threat. Remember that an "evaluation," by definition, wants to see and categorize what is already there. When one works toward a Schutzhund title, there will be some training to establish or enhance consistent behaviors. For the purposes of evaluation, there is no "training" at all. In fact, the handler needs to be very sure not to do anything to influence the dog's reactions. The entire goal is to expose the dog to carefully-constructed circumstances to watch his personality show itself.

Because the "protection" part is far less commonly understood, let's consider a few elements that are considered important in using the method to assess a dog's character. In all cases, the pertinent elements refer to adult dogs, not puppies or adolescents. Furthermore, the dog is being handled by his owner or regular trainer. That assumed, what does the evaluation with the helper show?

Threat Perception

The first time a sound dog sees this weird-looking person with a huge arm, he might be curious, but does not interpret him as threatening. In fact if he does, it's all over right there: a 60-second test has shown everything that anyone needs to know about that dog's potential for service work. For instance, if the dog takes one look at a motionless, silent human standing in a partially-hidden corner (the "blind"), and growls, threatens, tries to retreat, or, even worse, becomes seriously aggressive—I'd send him home without further ado. That is NOT a service dog temperament. However, if the candidate were to show general curiosity, or better yet, friendliness, he's worth a look. If he does, the helper would start teasing the dog, making enticing movements with his body and the sleeve (which might not be a sleeve at all, but only a big burlap tug roll) and allow the dog to grab and tussle like he would with any toy. A good service dog candidate would be quick to agree this is a great game. If he's worried about playing with a stranger, or won't get involved at all, that's not so good because he's showing either a lack of confidence or lack of initiative.

Inclination to Fight

Depending on the dog's initial response, the "game" might become more serious to get some additional information. If the dog is willing to tussle and play, then the stranger becomes a bit more willful and even threatening in his movements. Now the evaluation involves more questions. Does the dog lose interest in the game?

Get worried? Pick up and maintain eye contact with the stranger? Become aggressive? Have an emotional meltdown—cower, attempt to leave, urinate, or blow anal glands? Or does he not even notice the change in the helper's attitude? Perhaps the dog's behavior will change if you change the location, such as encountering the stranger in a dark parking lot where the dog has never been before. What if the stranger starts shouting or doing something unexpected? Adding this kind of pressure to the situation can show you some interesting things about the dog. (Remember that this is an evaluation, not training. Nobody should encourage any particular action from the dog. The handler must be completely neutral in order to see what the dog will do on his own.) When the dog is confronted by a stranger behaving weirdly, and even in mildly provoking ways, what might be his response? What answers you get reflect how quickly a dog might interpret fellow mall shoppers (often fairly weird!) or a nighttime jogger as a threat.

Desire to Catch

A different aspect—but also problematic for a service dog—would be a dog who is extremely quick to anticipate the fun or pleasure of catching "prey." It's not unusual for a service dog to encounter people in public who are afraid of him—especially children. Picture a frightened small child squealing and running away. Will the dog think "WOW!...Getitgetit!!!" and lunge for his prey? Many canines of many breeds will react exactly that way, because basic instincts tell them a fleeing, squealing mammal is lunch. A skilled helper can give off the right signals to convince a dog he is "prey." The questions about the dog, then, include: (1) how quick is he to become excited over the prospect of a chase? (2) will he remain biddable to the handler, despite excitement? (3) will he become so manic over the idea of a chase that he goes out of control and cannot be handled or commanded normally? If I see that a helper's first sudden twitch, lurch, or skittering away will launch the dog into grab/chase mode…this dog, also, is going home without further deliberation. Ideally, when the helper gives strong "chase me" signals, I'm looking for the dog who will yawn, glance at his wristwatch, look up at me, and say, "Hey, isn't it dinner time yet?' But remember this is the *third* phase of testing. The first two involved much willingness to work—therefore, I want this same dog who yawns over the helper to have no hesitation or difficulty working at other tasks (either with me or independently) in new circumstances with many distractions. Such dependability and versatility demonstrate the importance of the three phases of Schutzhund testing being used *together*.

Default Response

At the risk of being repetitious, I cannot overstress that when evaluating with a helper, as described above, I am not discussing a long, drawn-out process of months of sessions. Nor even so much that it becomes any more routine than normal task training or trips into public. Even if the dog considers the process a cool game, shows no tendency to get aggressive, and demonstrates that he's perfectly safe and predictable, you don't want him to develop the notion that every stranger he meets is there to play with him. That's not part of his job and will eventually frustrate everyone. A correct evaluation will expose the dog to the helper with approximately the same level of intensity wherein he might encounter a forklift at a warehouse retail store. "Well, what'dya know? Check this out, buddy! What do you think of this weird guy over here?" It happens. It passes. A skilled trainer watches keenly, does little, and observes reactions. Then the day's regular training resumes. The encounter might repeat a time or two, or even a few more, depending on the dog's responses, the individual circumstances, and what the trainer needs to see. But not so often that the process overshadows the frequency or importance of other service dog task training.

Reading Results

Please note that in no case should a Schutzhund-based evaluation be undertaken by novices, or even by skilled trainers without experience in this particular venue. Much experience is required to present the test conditions correctly, and also to read the dog's responses accurately. My ideal dog for a service dog candidate will either be oblivious—bored to tears with the whole concept—or else he'll refuse to believe the helper is anything but a buddy who likes to wrestle. When/if the game strengthens to an actual threat, he'll choose to back off or appease. But the helper's behavior must be deliberate and exact at any given moment to ensure correct reading of the dog and getting the information you need. The specific behavioral considerations are wide and varied, depending on the physical circumstances and the combined body language of the dog, helper, and handler—and even the particulars of the job for which you are screening.

JOB VARIETY

Different Personalities

Remember that this type of testing can be (and often is) used to evaluate a dog for more than a single kind of job! For a service dog, you're looking for one personality. Someone looking for a police patrol dog would be looking for something entirely different. The format of the test—carefully worked out and proven over nearly a century of use—will show you several important factors about a dog's character, personality, and soundness. For instance, a dog of highly desirable temperament for police work would consider the threat from the helper to be an active challenge of wits and skill.

This dog's mouth is the boxing gloves and the helper's sleeve is his punching bag. Right from the very beginning, his attitude to the helper is completely different from that of a good service dog candidate. A good police patrol candidate wants to dominate and subdue, not play.

Same Soundness

However, a good candidate for *either* job would not be worried about the new circumstances, the bystanders, other dogs he doesn't know, new and strange objects, or a funny-acting stranger. Any dog worried or hesitant about such things is showing you he is unsure of himself and consequently is a high risk for fear-biting in unexpected circumstances.

In line with what we discussed in Chapter 11 about more general tests of working in varied circumstances: so long as you're working an adult dog with his normal handler, it's the information you get in the beginning that is important. Over time, a skilled trainer can mask, emphasize, or redirect many of his dog's traits for the purpose of a title, or points in competition. An accurate evaluation needs to be based on what the dog shows before he becomes accustomed to a certain process or before it becomes a matter of routine.[3]

---

[3] Incidentally, the full value of the Schutzhund training process is that it contains a long series of new stressors and working conditions. As the dog continues to prove himself, he is continually moved up to additional challenges. A trainer has constant opportunity to evaluate his reactions to new circumstances and increasingly complex situations. Regardless of what titles the dog ever does or does not achieve, what strengths or weaknesses he displays (and there will a variety of both in almost any dog), or what competitions he might win, the process nets an enormous amount of information. Thus, a skilled, honest trainer/breeder who works successive generations of dogs through the extensive and demanding tasks gains substantial knowledge of his genetic line in a way that would be nearly impossible to duplicate elsewhere. His predictions about his adult dogs and about puppies from his own lines can become increasingly accurate. In particular, this is how the German Shepherd Dog was developed and is why the breed had such an enormously versatile reputation for so many years. In more recent years, the lack of such stringency and evaluation is precisely what is causing the plague of dangerous and nervous temperaments that are so prevalent today.

Trained Responses

Some years ago, because of my training background, I was asked to testify in a civil trial that involved a dog bite. The plaintiff was attempting to establish that Schutzhund work was dangerous in all aspects and should be automatic cause for a negative finding. All attorneys for both sides had been somewhat put off by watching a videotape (obtained from where, I never found out) of a very average-looking dog going through a third-phase test. They were trying to pin me down about whether or not I believed this video showed a dangerous dog. The defense attorney, in particular, could not seem to grasp the concept that the tape didn't really tell us anything of value—until I gave him a 90-second tutorial, and turned him loose with my own dog, Abby, and a baby-blue stuffed teddy bear. He discovered, right in the parking lot of his own office, that Abby would do a perfect "Schutzhund protection routine" for him (a stranger she'd never met) in order to obtain the little teddy bear she thought was so desirable. Incidentally, the "routine" included having him bang her on the head with his fist and slap her several times on both shoulders to see if she'd let go of the bear before she was told to. He gave me a completely blank look that showed the dawning of comprehension, and said, "She's doing exactly the same thing as the dog on the tape!" I heaved a large sigh of relief; we were making progress! The ensuing conversation kept edging closer to my goal:

"So is this all any dog is doing during Schutzhund protection? Playing a game?" he still wasn't sure.

"Not necessarily." I was still groping for the best words to explain.

"What does the protection routine tell you about the dog, then?" The attorney was still getting frustrated. "This dog is obviously completely safe to be around."

APPENDIX A: WHEN PERSONALITY MEETS CHARACTER

And she was. For Abby, "protection," as seen in Schutzhund competition, was, truly, a game she loved dearly. The leaping and barking at the helper with the sleeve was nothing more than the kind of action you see a trained horse doing in a movie to simulate a "fighting stallion." For Abby, nothing changed when the issue at stake was a 6-inch stuffed toy instead of a burlap sleeve. Is this true of all dogs doing Schutzhund? Not at all! A good police dog is ready and willing to fight a human for real. He has to be; his handler's life may depend on it. Some humans may suffer some confusion about this difference, but the dogs do not. In fact, even some police departments have learned the hard way that there are definite, specific differences in Schutzhund and actual patrol/protection training. It's not just a matter of perception. Not a few dogs trained with Schutzhund methods have been reported to prove the difference by galloping merrily alongside a fleeing crime perpetrator, watching alertly to see when he might decide to present the sleeve for a "bite."[4] When the sleeve isn't presented, the dog does nothing, and the perpetrator jogs off into the sunset.

But my point to the attorney was that it's often hard to tell the difference when you're looking at a dog who is merely performing the well-known routine after years of training. A very experienced trainer can pick up clues from the dog's body language, but for

---

[4] An interesting development of training technique is described in the book *Decoys And Aggression: A Police K9 Training Manual*, by Stephen A. Mackenzie (Calgary, Alberta: Temeron Books Inc., 1996.). Mackenzie is emphasizing the need for helpers to wear protective pants as well as the sleeve. Helpers training dogs without pants tend to lean down to let the dog get the sleeve—thereby protecting their legs. Some dogs trained this way were failing to halt suspects during real police work. The officers may have believed the dogs were being trained to attack, but the dogs were perfectly clear in their own minds that the concept was not about attacking the person. Once the specific routine changed and the sleeve wasn't offered in exactly the same way, no "bite" happened! As the author states, "Some [dogs] actually ran alongside, looking right at [the felon], as if they were wondering when he would slow up and bend down with the sleeve. They didn't bend and the dogs never bit them, allowing some to escape completely, much to the embarrassment of the K-9 units" (page 62).

the majority of observers, it's pretty difficult to tell. The valuable character information is to be found in the dog's initial reactions to newness, diversity, and moderate stress.

BASIC CONFIDENCE

For the doubtful, let's put the essence of the "protection" evaluation in a different context. If you don't see how the self-confidence and desire to play an interactive, all-stops-out game with a stranger tells you much about a dog's character, back up and consider something else you've probably already witnessed. Have you ever seen a dog who is normally a rambunctious, chewing, tugging playful companion at his own home turn into a picture of caution and worry when put into new surroundings? The vet's office. The dog park. A friend's house. The boarding kennel. A cross-country trip. The dog takes one look around at all the new circumstances (people, dogs, or whatever), and says, "Eeew, yuck. I think the spot right here between Mom's feet looks pretty good." Not love, money, treats, or toys can make him go play or act normally? What is this? This is the beginning of a peek at a dog's real character!

The next question broadens the peephole: if the situation is pressed, and the new circumstances begin getting closer and more "in his face," how will the dog react? Will he interpret a threat? Or possibly will he check first to see if the oncoming item is an invitation to play? Will he maintain control? Threaten or bite? Fall to pieces? Panic? Get nuts? Continue to obey commands? Can he stay focused on a sit or down if the handler asks for one? Friends, these are questions that need to be answered about a potential service dog. You need to know what the dog's genetic inclination will be, and also how controllable he will be despite the inclinations.

ESSENCE OF THE TEST

Ultimately, if the details above are confusing to you, boil it down to basics by remembering this: evaluating a "raw" dog with Schutzhund is only a matter of using a well-structured, time-tested forum for answering the questions raised in Chapter 11. Is it the only way to test a dog's temperament? Definitely not. But it's a very good way that gets a lot of undeserved bad press. Many excellent trainers use similar tactics—and may not even realize how similar their methods are. Regardless of what training methodology is used, such trainers have learned from experience the high value of knowing how a dog responds to stress. Those trainers develop procedures to expose a dog to stress and assess the reaction; they don't care what the method is called—they do it because it works. Schutzhund testing is one such method that's been in use for almost a century, and is a well-proven tool, especially for learning how a dog might react in more extreme circumstances, including direct provocation. Unlikely with a service dog, you think? Be careful betting on it. Over the years I've lost count of how many show-offs thought it would be funny to play boogeyman to my trainees—jumping at the dog, pretending to threaten, making growling noises.

Specific Assessments

Recapping the *process:* a three-phase Schutzhund evaluation assesses dog's ability to focus, search, and work independently among outside distractions (tracking); to obey and heed, close and at a distance, under distraction, pressure, the presence of people, other dogs, and varied, even annoying, stimuli (obedience); and to prove willingness to interact eagerly with known and unknown humans during excitement and some stress, to obey a handler despite mild outside provocation, and to refrain from aggression in neutral circumstances (protection).

Versatile Assessments

Recapping the *results:* the information sought in a Schutzhund assessment isn't a matter of obtaining (much less of stimulating) any specific behavior or reaction. You want the *dog* to show *you* his genetic inclinations in the face of challenging work circumstances, uncertainty, stress, and even provocation. This sort of test can be used to determine which dogs would be best for a wide variety of different kinds of jobs, service work being only one of them.

CAUTION

For anyone who might read the above paragraphs and be ready to rush out and buy a Schutzhund-titled dog to train as your service dog—*stop right there!* Don't. If you're reading carefully, you already know that is not what I am suggesting. A Schutzhund title is absolutely *not* a rubber-stamp temperament guarantee. Am I even advocating that you take your trainee to a Schutzhund club and join in the training process? No. Though I personally don't believe Schutzhund titles and service work are necessarily mutually exclusive, most clients don't need to spend either the extra time or money, and ultimately the potential is too high for creating focus problems and distractions from a service dog's primary work.

No, this appendix is not a blanket endorsement of Schutzhund dogs. Far less a recommendation that anyone needs to title a trainee. The purpose is to acquaint readers with the Schutzhund criteria and the concept of "proving" a dog through planned exposure to novelty and stress. If you intend to choose a service dog candidate from one of the classic protector breeds, you need to give much thought and research into how any particular breeder is assessing soundness and personality in his dogs.

As with any kind of training, different trainers use techniques differently, and with different goals. Any training tool—whether a prong collar, electric collar, choke collar, leash, kennel, or even treats—can be abused. Schutzhund is no different, and any Schutzhund evaluation is only as good as the trainer performing it. Most Schutzhund-titled dogs in the United States today are trained as a sport or as an exhibition of soundness in breeding stock. That doesn't mean it's not a very demanding type of training—it is! But, as discussed in Chapter 5 about obedience titles, the title alone does not tell you whether it was achieved through the quality of the dog or the quality of the training, or what combination thereof. In fact, the reverse is also true: some really good dogs can "show" poorly because the handler lacks skill or experience.

APPLICATION

Some trainers will be happy to tell you which dogs are naturals and which ones perform more because of training than character. Some trainers don't want to tell you this—probably because they're more interested in selling a dog than in your specific needs. How can you know the difference? It's not as hard as one might think—that's the process described in Chapter 11. However, when dealing with naturally protective breeds, I urge you to adopt a ruthless, rigid standard. If one single behavior from the dog raises a substantial question, send him back. Nothing is better than a good one; nothing is worse than a bad one.

If you plan to rely to any extent on a Schutzhund evaluation to choose your service dog, you should explain to the owner (whether breeder or re-seller) exactly what you are proposing to do with the dog and what kind of circumstances the dog might face in his working life. Let's use my own breed, the German Shepherd Dog, for an example. Suppose you are going to see a breeder/trainer who has a kennel full of German Shepherds, most of whom have been Schutzhund trained or tested. Among the comments you need to make are the ones below. We'll use some "technical terms" to help you make it very clear to the breeder. You are looking for the following:

- A very relaxed, low-energy dog.
- A dog that likes people. No aggression shown to strangers.
- Rock-solid nerve
- A *very* high threshold for perceiving a threat
- A dog with no dominance behavior to people or other dogs

Most dogs in most German Shepherd kennels (even good kennels!) are not going to fit this description. That doesn't necessarily make them bad dogs but merely incorrect for the job. In fact, the breeder may swoon and say, "Wow, you want a couch potato!" Actually, yes, by *his* terminology, you do. Service and guide dog programs who frequently and effectively use German Shepherds have created, as Fidelco says, "a breed within a breed."[5] But if this particular breeder says he has samples to show you, you need to return to Chapter 11, apply every syllable of the criteria there, and think up everything you can to see what the dog is made of.

Passing the Test

If you and/or an experienced trainer have made the decision to look into using Schutzhund work to evaluate service dogs, here are a few suggestions to clarify the process.

Let's suppose you are talking to a Schutzhund trainer and he tells you he understands all about the differences between competition and evaluation—he has dogs with wonderful temperaments. He says he understands exactly what you're looking for—dogs that are extremely reliable, very safe, very high threshold, very non-reactive. Well...super.

---

[5] You can visit the Fidelco Guide Dog Foundation online at *www.fidelco.org*.

This is a great starting point. If it's true, then he won't mind a bit if you ask for a demonstration. Ask him to bring out one of his samples of great temperament. Then suggest one or more (or all) of the following:

- "Let's get a child to run up to him and grab him around the neck."
- "Let's see some strangers approach him (rapidly) and reach out for him while you're looking the other way. No commands please. Let's just see what he does."
- What if I approach and actually bump into him? Or step on his paw?
- "Let's go visit a first grade classroom. You put the dog on a downstay and leave the room. I'll watch the dog."
- "I brought a dog with me that's the noisiest, most obnoxious little beast of a terrier I could find. We'll put the two dogs close together, let the terrier scream and fuss, and see if your dog makes any attempt to kill him. We'll also see if he'll still honor that down stay."
- "I have some Halloween masks in the car. Let's put them on a couple of adults—strangers—and see if your dog is approachable."
- "Let's have my friend over here walk up to your dog, talking normally, but carrying a BB gun or baseball bat on his shoulder. We'll have him casually swing it around a few times and see how your dog reacts."
- "Let's go find some joggers and see what he does when strangers are running toward him. Better yet, let's do this at night!"
- "Let's go sit on the sidelines at a tennis court, right near where people are swinging rackets, darting back and forth, and tossing balls. I want to see how your dog responds."

If the breeder backs off or starts making excuses, you're in the wrong place. These suggestions are exactly what YOU are proposing to do with a service dog. Someone who uses Schutzhund to evaluate correct temperament for service dogs should be completely comfortable with any of the above scenarios. If they know their business, and the dog has been accurately evaluated, the only response you're going to hear is "Sure, let's go." And the dog will pass every test with ease and confidence—no threat to anyone involved. The confidence you can have in such a candidate is one of the sweetest feelings in the dog world!

NEGATIVE ASSOCIATIONS

Let's return for a few moments to the various objections to Schutzhund in any form in connection with service dog work. You won't have to do much additional reading to discover that the word alone raises human hackles in most parts of the service dog community. Some groups have specific prohibitions against it in any form. Assistance Dogs International does not refer to Schutzhund training by name, but has a clause in their code of ethics reading, "An assistance dog may not be trained in a way to stimulate his prey instinct for guard or protection duty."[6]

This is a fairly common type of statement in service dog circles. Am I criticizing their intent of excluding dangerous training or temperament? No, I am not. Do I see any conflict between the type of evaluation I do and this Code of Ethics statement? No, I do not. For anyone who questions my support of, or believe in the value of, ADI, please reread Chapter 4 and Chapter 15. But this is an area in which semantics, misunderstandings, and even poor trainers all play roles.

Protection Training: NOT!

So far as various folks in the service dog community are professing concern about encouraging a trainee to attack a human, I could not possibly agree more. Rare (to the point of non-existence) is the service dog handler who would be qualified to manage such a dog. Furthermore a service dog's justification for being in public has absolutely *nothing* to do with protection. Lastly, no type of training should be given to any service dog that will endanger other people. However, to include Schutzhund *evaluation* in that category, is not merely incorrect, it's tossing out the proverbial baby with the

---

[6]Standards and Ethics Regarding Dogs, *www.assistancedogsinternational.com/mprogram.html*,.

bathwater. Schutzhund is an incredibly valuable tool to determine which dogs are *not* going to be dangerous in public.

One of the most important concepts I wish I could ingrain in the national service dog consciousness is that correct Schutzhund work, either as a test or as a sport, has absolutely nothing to do with establishing or increasing a dog's inclination to attack people, which would be the worst possible thing you could do with a service dog. Training a dog actually to attack a human requires different techniques than those used in Schutzhund, such as described earlier about some of the *faux pas* among police dogs when the criminals got away. I have been challenged many times with statements such as "I can't believe you're 'teaching that dog to bite.'"

Don't kid yourself. Every single dog in the world knows how to bite, and not a single one needed a human's help to figure it out, either. Proof fills emergency rooms across the country every week. Over the years, I've been chomped by a pretty wide variety of dogs. The very worst bite was from a Golden Retriever who went after me (yes, me, the German Shepherd person!) within a minute of our first meeting and had a credible try at removing my entire leg. This was a profoundly educational experience and contributed greatly to my convictions about needing to know, not just guess at, mental soundness in dogs. Conversely, one of my long-time fellow service dog trainers (of course…a Golden Retriever person!) took the worst bite of her life a few years ago from a German Shepherd. Ultimately, though breeds have general tendencies, breed alone will not tell you what you need to know. The best information is found by proving or disproving the soundness of an individual dog.

Confusion of Terms

Any experienced Schutzhund evaluator can tell you that a degree of misunderstanding is evident even from the terms used by some who object to the process. Objecting to the enhancement of "prey drive" is only one example. We already discussed earlier in this appendix how any dog with high or inappropriate amounts of "prey drive" ("drive" referring to "motivation") can certainly be a problem, especially with little children. But "prey drive" is only one aspect of canine personality that might motivate a dog to bite—or, for that matter, only one of several motivations used in actual protection training (non-Schutzhund) such as for police patrol work. Several other motivations play important—and far more serious—roles.[7] Prey drive is not the only potential problem. Dogs who have *any* of their "drives" out of balance will be dangerous in public, and they don't have to be encouraged by training, either! Those characteristics are innate. The entire purpose of this appendix is to highlight how Schutzhund can correctly identify those dogs in order to remove them from service selection.

Sporting Differences

In service dog work, danger resulting from an overlooked temperament problem is very real. Dogs already are what they are. In my opinion it is unfortunate that emphasis on Schutzhund as a competitive sport has, in recent years, tended to produce many dogs with extremely intense motivations of the kind that will score well, rather than with balanced working capability for different jobs. Such extremes have much to do with service dog advocacy groups' opposition to the entire concept of Schutzhund.

---

[7] For an in depth discussion of the variety of canine motivations, read the following two articles: *Let Me Tell You About My Dog*, Parts I and II, by Armin Winkler, online at *www.schutzhundvillage.com/terms1.html* and *www.schutzhundvillage.com/terms2.html*.

Personally, I have little patience with the Americanism of "more is better" where it concerns dogs, especially dogs bred and reared primarily to be pieces of sporting equipment. It's a serious error in assessing working temperament to assume that if a normal, functional amount of desire from a dog to grip and tug and tussle over a toy is good (which is completely common and desirable in any dog, especially in the retrievers who excel in service dog work)…then hyperactive, compulsive hysteria is better. Such a dog's manic tendencies might require three years of brainwashing before you can trust him off leash, but it will look incredibly energetic and flashy on a competition field. In fact, a handler might just win himself some huge trophies, but it doesn't make the dog a good prospect for an actual job.

PROTECTION DOGS ARE NOT SERVICE DOGS

I could not close this discussion without a brief mention of a new practice that has recently sprung up, a practice that is both incredibly dangerous and (so far as I can tell) quite far off base legally. In recent months I have read of certain groups who are training dogs to be aggressive and threatening in order to pair them with crime victims suffering Post Traumatic Stress Disorder or other challenges. Such groups are labeling these animals as service dogs. I cannot imagine how this could be justified. To qualify as service animals, a dog must actually mitigate the disability, not merely blockade the person.

Beyond that, any type of aggressive, protective behavior from a service dog in public is 100% unacceptable, legally or practically. Just a few weeks ago, I had a rousing conversation with another trainer about this concept. He stressed to me that such dogs weren't actually trained to bite, but only to sound off aggressively and threaten—which is a ludicrous distinction. (Aggressive behavior, by the way, is specifically mentioned by the Department of Justice as a valid reason to exclude a service dog from any given place.) Barking as a trained behavior for a specific purpose, such as for a signal or alert, is one thing, so long as it turns on and off on command. Actual aggressive threatening, complete with growls, advances, posturing, and hard eye contact, is entirely another matter. Any trainer worth his salt knows that aggression is not a static characteristic. It either minimizes or it grows: if it's okay to growl and threaten today, the dog is highly likely to assume it's okay to bite later.

While I am extremely sympathetic to crime victims—and in fact probably agree that some of them would be well-served by a personal protection dog, such a dog should not be confused with a service dog. If you are interested in learning more and reading diverse opinions, the IAADP has two articles on their web site that are helpful and informative from the technical and mental health points of view.[8] However, I raise the example here primarily as a means of clarifying what I am *not* recommending.

CONCLUSION

What I *am* recommending is to obtain the best, most thorough knowledge possible about any dog you are considering for service work. If you are considering dogs from among the protective breeds, pay extra attention to how the breeder screens his candidates for all types of jobs. Most of the best use some form of Schutzhund-based testing. Don't assume they're creating "attack dogs!" They might be doing nothing more than figuring out which dogs have short fuses—and which don't. Understand everything you can about the process and factor it into your prerequisites for

---

[8] *Disaster is Not What a Trauma Victim Needs*, by Natalie Sachs-Ericsson is online at www.iaadp.org/ptsd.html and *How Many Things Do You Find Wrong With This Picture*, at www.iaadp.org/attack.htm.

safe temperament in your training candidate. How your potential purchase reacts to variety, novelty, and moderate stress is hugely important. Not only may your working relationship with the dog be at stake, but also potentially the safety of others around you. In my opinion, if more extensive temperament testing were properly utilized by more service dog trainers, we would see a higher success ratio and far fewer problems on the street during the dogs' working lives.

Not too long ago, after my father died, my mother faced the reality of living by herself for the first time in her life. Her hearing is very poor, and she lives in a remote area. She wanted a household companion dog, one who would alert her to the presence of outsiders and/or if something was wrong in the house, and provide a discouraging presence to vandals or schemers. At the same time, Mom's house is often full of grandchildren and (very young) great-grandchildren. Other small dogs are present. There are chickens in the back yard. People come and go. Gates get left open. Neighbors pop in for visits. Any large dog entering the home had to be a no-risk, no-exceptions candidate. Now…putting a dog into a complex home situation does *not* equal the task of choosing a service dog, but there are important parallels in choosing a predictable, safe temperament. Anybody want to guess what I went shopping for? To me, it was a no-brainer. I went to a skilled breeder/trainer who I knew used Schutzhund tests to evaluate dogs, told her exactly what I needed, and bought (sight unseen from 1,000 miles away) an adult, spayed female German Shepherd, Frigga vom Oberen Lechsee. "Frigga" had already earned a Schutzhund I title through the United Schutzhund Clubs of America and her parents and ancestors were all similarly tested and titled, either in the United States or in Germany. It took about 30 minutes to acclimate Frigga to Mom's household. The process was totally uneventful, and her trustworthiness in all circumstances has been 100%. My mother is not an experienced trainer, yet I would defy anyone, any program, or any criteria, to evaluate this dog and call her unsafe. What she is, in fact, is *proven*—a characteristic that I wish was far more common in our canine world today.

SUGGESTED READING

German Shepherd Dog Club of America: Working Dog Association. *What is Schutzhund?* 20 May 2005 <*www.gsdca-wda.org/schutzhund.htm*>

Hilliard, Steward. "Character," *The German Shepherd Book,* Susan Barwig and Asa Mays, eds. (Wheat Ridge, CO: Hoflin Publishing), pp. 66-81. This entire book is highly recommended.

Hilliard, Stewart and Sue Barwig. *Schutzhund, Theory and Training Methods.* (Hoboken, NJ: Howell Book House), 1991.

Tiz, Joy. *The Elements of Temperament.* 20 May 2005. <http://www.dogstuff.info/elements_of_temperament_what_is_temperament.html>. This is probably the best written explanation of canine "nerve" that I have seen.

Index

A

abuse, 69, 174
accommodation, 159, 164
aggression, 185
aggressive, 153, 214, 230
alert, 184
American Kennel Club, 42, 47, 119, 195
Americans with Disabilities Act, 10, 33, 163
assistance dog, 8
Assistance Dogs International (ADI), 11, 40, 192, 194
Assistive Search Alert (ASA), 179
Australian Shepherds, 127, 171
autism, 95, 180

B

Begleithund (BH), 42, 211
Belgian Malinois, 125, 127, 205
Belgian Shepherds, 205
BH, *See* Begleithund
bites, 105, 108, 143, 146, 153, 205, 218, 219
boot camp, 55
Border Collies, 127, 171
Bouviers, 125, 127
Boxers, 125, 205
breed selection, 115, 117, 120, 223
breeders, 115, 137, 139, 140, 186, 206
breeds, 78, 123, 205
budget, 28, 194, 199, 201

C

certification, 32, 34, 37, 40, 43
  of dogs, 32, 34
  of trainers, 32, 36

children, 64, 103, 113
clickers, 49
client, 9, 153
Companion Dog (competitive title), 42, 195
companion dog (job classification), 8, 104, 110, 112
competence, 46
competition, 207
contracts, 42, 112, 165
corrections, 49, 59, 60, 65, 68, 69, 71, 75, 78
curriculum, 55

D

Delta Society, 20, 40
Department of Justice, 7, 33
Dobermans, 125, 205
dominance, 116

E

electric collar, 49, 72
employment, 162
equipment, 46, 48, 57, 114, 120, 166
evaluating
  clients, 6, 48, 50, 71, 81, 121
  dogs, 43, 71, 119, 147, 149, 151, 221, 225
  trainers, 41, 45, 53, 100, 118, 199

F

fetch, 17, 70
  See also retrieve
fighting dogs, 131
Flat Coat Retrievers, 123

INDEX

G
genetic disease, 118, 122, 133, 140
German Shepherds, 125, 127, 185, 205, 206, 228
German Shorthaired Pointers, 129
Golden Retrievers, 123, 228
guide dog, 8, 11

H
handler, 9
harness, 121, 182
hearing assistance dog, 8, 11, 97
home, 10
Hounds, 128

I
insurance, 114, 158
International Association of Assistance Dog Partners, 18, 165

J
jobs, 14, 77, 78, 83, 89, 91, 98

K
kennel, 10, 55

L
Labrador Retrievers, 123
liability, 107, 113, 114, 158

M
major life activity, 12, 163
Malinois, *See* Belgian Malinois
Minimum Performance Test, 41, 43, 194
mixed breeds, 132
motivation, 54, 69
   See also rewards
Multiple Sclerosis, 12

O
obedience trials, 42

P
pack behavior, 107
parents, 9, 64, 108, 109, 153
personality, 207, 213, 217
phone retrieve, 68
   See also telephone
Pointers, 128
police K9, 11
Post Traumatic Stress Disorder, 12, 17, 230
prey drive, 70, 215, 229
program, 9
prong collars, 49, 78
protection, 19, 209, 221
protective, 126, 185, 206, 210, 230
psychiatric, 17
public, 8, 10, 12, 26, 40, 42, 64, 113
pulling a wheelchair, 14
puppies, 56, 107, 125, 186

R
registration, 195
rescues, 135, 137
resident therapy dog, 8
Resident Therapy Dogs, 170
retrieve, 85
   See also fetch
rewards, 61, 62
   See also motivation
Rottweilers, 125, 127, 205

S
Schnauzers, 125
Schutzhund, 206, 209, 220, 227, 232
search, 67, 179, 183, 208
seizure, 17, 92, 98
   alert, 92, 93, 94, 99
   response, 92, 94

self-training, 55, 161
service animal, 7
service dog, 8, 112
Setters, 128
Shetland Sheepdogs, 127
size, 121
socializing, 149, 153
sponsors, 9, 45, 117, 130, 142, 153, 192, 197, 200, 201, 202
sport, 66
stress, 143, 150, 154, 221
Supreme Court, 162

T

tasks, 14, 77, 78, 83, 89, 91, 98
teaching, 83, 90, 91, 96
telephone, 14, 78, 82
See also phone retrieve
temperament, 116, 133, 151, 154, 156, 214

Terriers, 130
testing
  performance, 46, 47, 119, 155, 193, 196
  temperament, 144, 146, 147, 205, 214, 226
Therapy Dogs International, 169
toy breeds, 132
trainee, 10, 23, 161
trainer, 9

U

United Kennel Club, 42, 47, 195
United Schutzhund Clubs of America, 42, 195, 232

W

Working Dog Association, 42, 195

About the Author

Julie Nye's fascination with dog training began in early childhood with family pets and working farm dogs. A native of Hessel, Michigan, college and employment moved her to the Greenville, South Carolina, area in 1981. Recruited from the ranks of competitive obedience trainers, she began formal involvement with the Dogs for Disabled program as a volunteer in the early 1990s. Her work with that program progressed to training, public demonstrations and education, board involvement, and is currently that of Executive Director. Her undergraduate degree in publishing and graduate work in education have proven complementary to efforts with assistance dogs.

Julie lives on a small farm in Easley, South Carolina, and enjoys the company of three Plantation Tennessee Walking Horses, several goats, a colony of barn cats, and of course several dogs, including four German Shepherds, one Boston Terrier, one Sheltie, and one Labrador who is a retired assistance dog. *Practical Partners* is her fourth book, and the first in the assistance dog venue.